Toronto

Front cover: Toronto skyline

Right: CN Tower

TOP 10 ATTRACTIONS

CN Tower •
The city's high
spot, with
fantastic views
(page 33)

Niagara Falls • One of Canada's most awesome and iconic
attractions *(page 64)*

Old Town • The Flatiron
Building in the St Lawrence
Market area *(page 40)*

Little Italy • Discover a
lively neighborhood with chic
boutiques, authentic cafes and
restaurants *(page 58)*

Art Gallery of Ontario • Features the work of Henry Moore and many Canadian artists *(page 45)*

Chinatown • Part of the city's great ethnic mix, this is the place to come for a taste of Asia *(page 47)*

Queen Street West • A funky shopping district *(page 42)*

Toronto Islands • There are few more stunning vistas than the city skyline from this favorite summer destination *(page 30)*

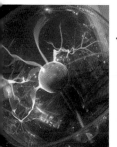

Ontario Science Centre • Discover what's hot in science and technology *(page 59)*

Royal Ontario Museum • Undergoing a massive transformation, it's renowned for a superb Chinese collection *(page 51)*

6

CONTENTS

104

37

11

93

80

INTRODUCTION

Canada's largest city (pop 2.5 million in the Greater Toronto Area or GTA) is also, according to world-renowned urban planner, Jane Jacobs, 'a city that works'. It is ideally placed on the northwest shore of Lake Ontario, easternmost of the Great Lakes that connect to the North Atlantic via the St Lawrence Seaway. The province of Ontario has its seat of government here and though Ottawa, four hours' drive away, is the nation's capital, Toronto is its cultural, entertainment and financial heart. A quarter of the country's population lives within a 160-km (100-mile) radius of the city. Niagara and the US border are just 90 minutes away, and half the population of the US is within a day's drive or an hour's flight.

On the same latitude as the French Riviera and one degree north of Boston, Toronto has the warmest spring and summers in the country, helped by the moderating effect of Lake Ontario. In winter the temperature is just below freezing, dipping in January, with around 10cm (4in) of snow, making it a place for both winter and summer activities.

Skyscraper City

Toronto once had a reputation as a conservative backwater, rolling up the sidewalks at 6pm on Sunday, but the last two decades of the 20th century saw an enormous revitalization take place, with striking new architecture, thriving theater and culture, and terrific dining and shopping, making it a kind of miniature New York without the hassles or perils.

To some people, this transformation seems like a miracle. Certainly so when you realize that the tallest building in the city in 1972 was still the Royal York, at a mere 19 floors.

Toronto's modern skyline

Now the city has some of the tallest buildings in the world, international architects compete for tenders, and awards continue to encourage local excellence in design.

Peace and Order

Despite its sudden rush to fame and modernity, the Canadian emphasis on 'Peace, Order, and Good Government' still shows. Old and new blend together: metal and glass skyscrapers abut Renaissance Revival beauties, glass shopping malls overlook sturdy Victorian churches, old Victorian residences stand facing large apartment complexes. But through all of the development Torontonians have fought to ensure that Downtown remains residential, although many of the historic industrial buildings there are now being converted into office spaces as well as residential lofts. The subways are relatively safe and clean. People speak in quiet tones in restaurants and most other public places, and don't tend to rush around jostling and poking each other with their elbows. There is little that disturbs the peace.

But the people are passionate about their sport, especially ice hockey. There's a standing joke that the only place you'll see Torontonians approaching disorder or enthusiasm is at a Leafs game, when the home team is on a roll. They are also passionate about their cultural heritage. Go into any bookstore and you're likely to see a special section devoted to Canadian authors, film-makers and other famous Canucks. And there's no doubt that Torontonians keep a keen eye on

The Hockey Hall of Fame

Take a break

their larger neighbor to the south, which may account for the many Canadians who have succeeded in the American comedy industry. Living so close to a giant gives them a (sometimes caustic) perspective on its quirks, inconsistencies and hypocrisies.

Getting Around

Physically, Toronto looks like an American city. The streets are laid out in a grid (with some minor deviations), but they have names instead of numbers, with Yonge Street, the longest street in the world, running back from the Harbourfront 1,896km (1,178 miles) northwest to reach the US border in Minnesota.

If you arrive at Lester B. Pearson International airport and take a taxi into the city, you'll sweep by the glorious lakeshore – the first thing you'll see is the CN Tower shooting up to the stars and a cluster of tall buildings that make up the skyline.

Downtown the streets are clogged with traffic; streetcars operate along their tracks; and, depending on the weather, people either sun themselves at cafés and pocket parks or huddle down below in the underground city, protected from the cold – a continuous underground pedestrian system connects 27km (17 miles) of shopping, services and entertainment.

A Diverse Community

So how did this stodgy city inhabited by conservative Wasps who dined at home or at their club become the city that it is today? The answer is immigration. Before World War II there were small communities of Jewish, Chinese and Italian

Eminent Torontonians

Scientists **Frederick G. Banting** and **Charles H. Best** discovered insulin in 1921, while working at the University of Toronto. **Dr Murray Barr** contributed important work to the determination of sex by cell analysis, and **James Collip** isolated the hormone ACTH.

Distinguished writer **Robertson Davies** (1913–95) has long been associated with the city, although he was born in Peterborough, England. **Morley Callaghan** worked briefly with Ernest Hemingway at the *Toronto Daily Star* and followed him to Paris where he wrote *That Summer in Paris* (for The Literary Scene, see page 21).

In the musical world, **Glenn Gould** (1932–82) is still recognized as one of Bach's greatest interpreters. **The Band**, **Blue Rodeo**, **Rush**, **Neil Young**, **The Barenaked Ladies**, and chanteuse, **Feist**, are some of the singers and groups whose careers were launched in Toronto.

Film stars hailing from Toronto have included **Mary Pickford** (whose house is a landmark on University Avenue), **Raymond Massey** and **Jason Robards, Jr**, both of whom came from distinguished Toronto families. Film directors **Norman Jewison** and **David Cronenberg** also grew up in Toronto.

Carnival time gives the city a Caribbean flavor

people and much larger communities of English, Irish, and Scottish and Scottish-Irish. In the 1950s, new immigrants began to arrive. They came from Eastern Europe, from Italy, from Hong Kong, from the Caribbean, Central America, Vietnam, India and Pakistan. During the separatist troubles in Québec in the 1970s, people also came from Montréal. Drawn by the wealth of the city, they brought their culture.

Today, foreign-born residents comprise more than 44 percent of population and it has been estimated that more than 100 languages are spoken, one third of the residents speaking at home a language other than English. Unlike the US, which likes to think that all new arrivals head straight into the melting pot, Canada has adopted a framework that supports a genuine multi-ethnic society. At school, children learn about their neighbors' cultures and an attempt is made to understand and appreciate differences in cultural heritage.

This cultural diversity makes any visit to Toronto fascinating and the patchwork of different neighborhoods and villages, with great dining and shopping, are worth seeking out: the five Chinatowns, including the downtown one at Dundas and Spadina; Kensington Market, now mostly Caribbean; farther west along Dundas, the Portuguese; Lawrence and Avenue Road Jewish communities; Roncesvalles in the West End for the Eastern Europeans and Russians; Danforth in the East End for Greeks; Gerrard Street East between Greenwood and Coxwell for South Asian culture; and the Little Italys, along College Street between Euclid and Shaw, and along St Clair West.

Cultural Appeal

This patchwork is just the background to your visit. In the foreground are the many singular attractions of the city. If you appreciate fine art, you'll want to see the collections of Canadian (including Inuit) and European art at the Art Gallery of Ontario, which also has one of the largest collections of Henry Moore anywhere.

You'll want to browse in the galleries in Yorkville and on Queen Street West, and visit the McMichael Canadian Art Collection to see the famous works by Canada's Group of Seven. The Royal Ontario Museum has another prime

Lakeshore Highlights

Do make sure to go down to the lakeshore – Toronto's Harbourfront is one of the most imaginative developments of its sort anywhere in the world. Old warehouses and factories have been converted into galleries, theaters, shopping complexes, restaurants, craft studios, and more. And you can actually get out on the water, aboard cruise boats, schooners, canoes, and kayaks.

collection – don't miss their Chinese and Korean galleries, or their Canadiana galleries. The life-science exhibits here are also extraordinary. Across the street, the Gardiner Museum of Ceramic Art has an amazing collection, and just around the corner on Bloor Street, the Bata Shoe Museum is unique.

Outdoor Attractions

Toronto has an impressive waterfront on Lake Ontario and is unique in having a cluster of islands just across the harbor. Board the ferry, at the foot of Bay Street, with a bicycle and a picnic and ramble along the bosky

Out on the lake

walkways: You won't believe that you're only 10 minutes from a large city. The landmark Ontario Place is another highly imaginative waterfront park (with outdoor theater, open only in summer) on the Lakeshore west of downtown.

In the Don River Valley, the Science Centre draws millions, and with good reason. There are more than 400 interactive exhibits that elucidate physics, biology and chemistry, with exciting demonstrations daily. The Toronto Zoo is another forward-looking institution where the animals are free to roam in paddocks or pavilions that replicate entire natural habitats, from the rocks, soil and climate to the flora and other fauna.

And anyone with children is liable to be dragged off to experience the roller coasters operating at Canada's Wonderland.

Bright Nightlife

The city offers plenty to do in the evenings, too. Try to catch a show at Second City or one of the other comedy clubs. You can enjoy Broadway-style shows at a fraction of the price at such theaters as the spectacular Princess of Wales, the historic Royal Alexandra, Pantages, or the Elgin and Winter Garden. Many small Canadian theater companies thrive here; their talents can be seen most easily at the Fringe Festival in June. Toronto has some terrific arts companies, such as The National Ballet of Canada.

Musically, the city also has rich pickings. Besides the Toronto Symphony, it supports many smaller, internationally known groups like Tafelmusik, the Canadian Brass, and the great Mendelssohn Choir.

For sports fans there's baseball at Rogers Centre, and hockey, football and basketball at the Air Canada Centre.

Bright lights, big city

A BRIEF HISTORY

Little is known about Toronto's early history, except that the plain between the Humber River in the west and the Don in the East was used by Canada's First Nations (indigenous groups) as a stopping place on the Toronto Trail between the Lower and Upper Great Lakes. The first European to travel along this route was Etienne Brulé in 1615. He had been sent by Samuel Champlain to establish a lucrative fur trade, focusing on beaver to satisfy the European craving for beaver hats. It was another 105 years, though, before the first trading post, Fort Toronto, was established to intercept British rivals carrying furs across Lake Ontario to New York State. The first post was replaced in 1751 with Fort Rouillé, whose foundations are etched in cement on Exhibition Place.

New France

The French explored much of North America's interior, including the Mississippi, attracted by the mineral and timber resources and also by the opportunity to convert the First Nations to Christianity. They established such cities as Detroit, St Louis, and New Orleans. The British, who were founding settlements along the East Coast from Maine to Georgia, were seen as a threat to the French. In 1670, the British established the Hudson's Bay Company and the rivalry between the two powers increased, leading eventually to war. In 1758, the British marched on Fort Frontenac, outmanoeuvering the French for an easy victory; they took Fort Niagara the following year. When the news reached the French, they burned down Fort Rouillé to keep it from British hands.

A siege was begun against Québec City. On the night of 12 September 1759, General James Wolfe managed to sneak

4,500 British soldiers behind the city's defenses, surprising the French and their leader, the Marquis de Montcalm. The ensuing battle on the Plains of Abraham was brief and bloody. Both leaders perished: Wolfe survived long enough to hear of his victory. Montcalm died a few hours later. After five days, Québec surrendered. The 1763 Treaty of Paris effectively cut off any French ambitions for rule in Canada.

Muddy York and the 1812 War

The American Revolution established a potentially hostile nation just across Lake Ontario, making Toronto a significant strategic stronghold, a fact quickly recognized by the

The Loyalists

The Canadian rallying cry of 'Peace, Order, and Good Government' contrasts with America's 'Life, Liberty, and the Pursuit of Happiness.' This love of order is the legacy of the Loyalists in the 13 rebel colonies who abandoned their property and fled the chaos of the American Revolution. They came from every class and walk of life, united in their loyalty to the Crown. Regarded as traitors in the rebel colonies, they were harassed, beaten up, tarred and feathered, and often driven from their communities. They forfeited their voting rights, were unable to sell land or recover debts, and were denied their livelihood. After the American victory they were left with only one course of action: exile. Eighty thousand fled the colonies, about half to England and the British West Indies. The rest came to Canada. In 1783, around 30,000 sailed to Nova Scotia, tripling its population. Thousands trekked by ox cart and on foot to the St Lawrence River and the shores of Lake Ontario. Many were ill-equipped to deal with the rigors of frontier life, and many died. In 1789, Britain announced that those who had remained loyal were entitled to add the letters UE (United Empire) to their names, a privilege extended to their families and descendants.

British administration. In 1793, Lieutenant Governor John Graves Simcoe arrived to build a settlement named York that he believed would not only secure Lake Ontario, but also provide easy access to Lake Huron and the interior. A garrison was built and streets were laid out in a 10-block rectangle around King, Front, and Berkeley streets. A 53-km (33-mile) oxcart trail leading north was named Yonge Street. Thus was born muddy

Traders inspect a fur

York, which became the capital of Upper Canada when parliament met in 1797. It prospered, and by 1812 had a population of 703.

Simcoe's settlement was soon put to the test. British attempts to disrupt America's Atlantic trade routes led to the War of 1812; the Americans invaded Canada, taking advantage of the weak British forces, most of whom were away fighting Napoleon in Europe. In fact, there were only 1,600 British soldiers, led by Major-General Sir Isaac Brock, available to defend Upper Canada. Brock did win some early victories, notably at Fort Michilimackinac, where Lake Huron meets Lake Michigan. He also managed to beat the Americans back along the Niagara Frontier in October 1812, but he died in the process, which was a major blow to the British forces.

In April 1813, 14 American ships carrying 1,700 troops landed in York; they burned the Parliament Buildings and the fort. The British retreated, leaving John Strachan to

The 19th-century re-enacted in Black Creek Pioneer Village

negotiate a peace. The war finally ran out of steam, and was officially ended with the Treaty of Ghent in 1814, though skirmishes continued along the borders for years.

Growth and Consolidation

After the war trade revived, the city grew and thrived under the conservative direction of the so-called Family Compact, a government elite, many of whom were or had been Loyalists. Their names still echo around Toronto to this day – William Jarvis, John Beverley Robinson, William Warren Baldwin, and D'Arcy Boulton.

Their power was undermined slowly but surely during the 19th century as the city grew, attracting a more diverse population of immigrants from Ireland and Scotland who challenged the Family Compact's self-satisfied, pro-British, Tory and Anglican assumptions. Revolutionary transportation developments opened up the city further, allowing new ideas and influences to enter the country. The Erie Canal was extended to Oswego on Lake Ontario and the Welland Canal cut through the Niagara Peninsula so that Toronto was linked to New York State and points west. In 1834 the city was incorporated and the name York was changed to Toronto, a Native Canadian word for 'meeting place.'

Immigrant Agitators

Immigrants continued to pour in, primarily from the British Isles, and Irish immigration became a tidal wave that would last for almost 20 years. Among the immigrants were agitators who launched radical papers such as the *Canadian Freeman* and demanded reform. William Lyon Mackenzie, publisher of the *Colonial Advocate*, became one of the most famous when he fomented a rebellion in 1837. His 700 rebels gathered at Montgomery's Tavern on Yonge Street, near today's Eglinton Avenue, and began marching downtown, intending to overthrow the government. The sheriff called out the militia, who scattered the rebels at Carlton Street and pursued them back to the tavern. Mackenzie fled south across the border. His fellow conspirators, Lount and Matthews, were caught and hanged.

The British parliament took note of the discontent, appointing Governor-General Lord Durham, who recommended 'anglification' as a solution for both Upper and Lower Canada. In 1841, Great Britain created the United Province of Canada – comprising Upper and Lower Canada – as a concession to the people's desire for more independence. William Lyon Mackenzie was allowed to return home and in fact became the city's first mayor.

Between 1834 and the turn of the century, a major industrial city was built with the help of Toronto's many new arrivals. Water, gas and electricity were installed. A public transportation system was established and municipal

Bustling Yonge Street, 1901

buildings were erected, including St Lawrence Hall (1851) and the Toronto Stock Exchange (1852). The pace increased after the railroads arrived in the 1850s; Toronto was then able to take advantage of trading routes to the US and also of its position as capital of the newly formed province of Ontario. The province had been established when the Dominion of Canada was created on 1 July 1867, joining Ontario, Québec, New Brunswick, and Nova Scotia in Eastern Canada.

Although the country's first prime minister, Sir John A. Macdonald, had a vision of a nation stretching from ocean to ocean, Ontarian Oliver Mowat ensured that the provinces kept some autonomy. Born in Kingston, Ontario, of Scottish parents, Mowat was elected premier of Ontario in 1872. For the next 24 years he fought many battles to secure sovereign rights for provincial parliaments. As a result, the provinces have to this day retained a great deal of autonomy.

The population tripled between 1871 and 1891, rising to 181,000. Toward the end of the 19th century, Canada, already profiting from lumber and agriculture, started to exploit its formidable mineral potential. Oil was struck around the southern tip of Lake Huron; copper and nickel were discovered at Copper Cliff and Sudbury in 1883; subsequently silver and gold were found as well. Meanwhile, travel and commerce had been enhanced by the completion in 1885 of the Canadian Pacific Railway, which linked the east and west coasts – a stunning feat of engineering and sheer human willpower and drive.

A Wealthy Elite

Commerce was creating such wealthy merchants as Timothy Eaton and Robert Simpson, and such utility magnates and financiers as Henry Pellat, the creator of Casa Loma. The boom fueled more construction. In 1890, distiller George Gooderham built his mansion at St George and Bloor (the York Club today). The completion of the Provincial Parliament buildings followed (1886–92) and old City Hall

The Literary Scene

Toronto has bred more than its fair share of famous authors, from internationally acclaimed writers such as Margaret Atwood and Michael Ondaatje, to the newer crop of talent such as Rohinton Mistry and Anne Marie MacDonald (who both catapulted to fame after their novels were picked by Oprah's now-defunct book club).

A multiethnic group, Toronto authors have brought mythic stories from other countries and have immortalized the city through their work. Ascribing symbolic value to Toronto, writers such as Michael Ondaatje described the building of the Bloor Street Viaduct and the Harris Filtration Plant in detailed lyrical prose in The English Patient prequel, In the Skin of a Lion. Other Toronto authors such as Anne Michaels, Barbara Gowdy, Nino Ricci, Michael Redhill and André Alexis have followed suit. The result is that the city has a rich literary scene that includes endless readings and festivals.

Toronto's annual International Festival of Authors in October is the culminating event of the year-round program of readings at the Harbourfront Centre.

at Queen and Bay opened in 1899. The new moneyed folk, however, still subscribed to the British way of life, supporting the Queen and her Empire, patronizing private clubs, and enjoying the sporting life. Little had rocked the social foundations that had been laid down in the 18th century. It would take the arrival of more immigrants, increased industrialization, and a war to accomplish that.

Boom, Bust, and a New Society

The booming economy attracted more immigrants, only now they came from Italy and from Jewish communities throughout Eastern Europe, and they settled in their own ethnic enclaves; the Italians around College and Grace and the Jewish around the Kensington Market. By 1911, more than 30,000 of the city's population were foreign-born. Torontonian culture expanded as well, with the opening of the landmark Royal Ontario Museum in 1912.

The Old City Hall reflected in a modern skyscraper

Toronto sent 70,000 men to the trenches in World War I and provided much of the industrial power needed to support the war – including airplanes, ships, and other military supplies. After the war, manufacturing and factory industries continued to expand. Automobiles, first built locally by the Canada

Cycle and Motor Company some 12 years earlier, began to appear regularly on the streets of Toronto. The mining boom brought more money to Bay Street financiers.

But times were not all good for all people. Nativism erupted against immigrants in Canada in the 1920s and 1930s just as it had in the United States. Canadian newspapers complained that Canada had become the 'dumping ground for the scum of Europe.' In 1923, the Canadian Chinese Exclusion Act was passed, and throughout the 1920s Jews were accused of being Bolsheviks and Communists. The Depression only intensified the discrimination against Jews, making it a common Canadian practice, but as the intent of the Nazi war machine became clear, people's attitudes softened, and, when Canada went to war, were swallowed in an effort to save the world for democracy.

After the war, the discovery of uranium in Ontario sparked a second mining boom and a long economic expansion that helped establish the suburbs and the affluent consumer society of the 1950s. The Chinese Exclusion Act was repealed in 1947; then, under pressure from the United Nations, Toronto opened its doors to all immigrants, and skilled and energetic newcomers from Greece, Poland, China, Pakistan, Italy and the Caribbean transformed the stolid city of Toronto.

Although the socially prominent conservative elite still dominated the banks and boardrooms, it became easier for newcomers to enter politics. Nathan Phillips, the city's first Jewish mayor, was elected in 1954. At the beginning of the 1950s, 31 percent of the population was foreign-born; by 1962 this figure had reached 42 percent.

The trend continued, and as more immigrants arrived they changed the face and attitude of the city, along with the Montréalers who came to Toronto in the 1970s. The Parti Québecois had sought to separate Québec from Canada for a long time, but during this decade the antipathy between French-and English-speaking citizens intensified to the point that many non French-speaking Montréalers fled to Toronto.

A Megacity

The other mark of the decade was that of explosive growth. Skyscrapers shot up at Bloor and Yonge and in the Financial District. In 1971 Ontario Place was built; in 1972 restoration began at Harbourfront, and the Toronto Zoo and the Science Centre opened in 1974. The city's signature landmark, the CN Tower, opened in 1975, followed by the SkyDome (now Rogers Centre) in 1989, and in the 1990s the Princess of Wales Theatre, the CBC Building, and the Air Canada Centre were built. Toronto's architectural landscape continues to evolve, with a major expansion of the Art Gallery of Ontario and the Royal Ontario Museum, the construction of the Four Seasons Centre for the Performing Arts, as well as the Ontario College of Art and Design – built on stilts.

In 1998, against strong local opposition, the suburbs of Etobicoke, East York, North York, York and Scarborough merged with Toronto to make a megacity, the fifth largest in North America.

A pencil box college building

Toronto the Good, the city that rolled up the sidewalks at 6pm, closed shop on Sundays, and for 20 years did not have one friendly neighborhood bar open on Sunday, had gone. But, overall, the city has only gained from the contributions that its ethnic groups have made – in dining, literature, music, and political life.

Historical Landmarks

1615 Etienne Brulé explores the Toronto Trail. Fort Rouillé built.

1763 Treaty of Paris ends French ambitions for Canadian rule.

1791 Upper and Lower Canada established.

1793 Col. John Graves Simcoe names Upper Canada settlement York.

1812 The War of 1812.

1824 Welland Canal opens, linking Lake Erie and Lake Ontario.

1834 City incorporated, named Toronto.

1837 Rebellion led by William Lyon Mackenzie.

1841 United Province of Canada established.

1840s–50s Mass Irish immigration.

1851 St Lawrence Hall built.

1852 Toronto Stock Exchange opens.

1858 Storm creates Toronto Islands.

1867 Canadian Confederation; Toronto becomes capital of Ontario.

1886 Construction begins on Provincial Parliament buildings.

1893 First Stanley Cup played.

1906 First autos built by Canada Cycle and Motor Company.

1914–18 World War I. More than 13,000 Torontonians killed in battle.

1920 Group of Seven's first art exhibit.

1947 Cocktail lounges permitted.

1959 St Lawrence Seaway opened by Elizabeth II and Eisenhower.

1965 New City Hall built.

1970s Harbourfront developed; CN Tower built.

1998 Suburbs amalgamated into a megacity.

1999 Last hockey game at Maple Leaf Gardens. Air Canada Centre opens.

2005 Twelve years of Liberal rule ends with a vote of no confidence. The Conservatives win 2006 election and lead a minority government.

2006 The Four Seasons Centre for the Performing Arts opens.

2007 The Royal Ontario Museum (ROM) unveils the Michael Lee Chin Crystal, the centerpiece of its new addition designed by Daniel Libeskind.

2008 Art Gallery of Ontario (AGO) re-opens following a multimillion-dollar expansion by architect, Frank Gehry.

WHERE TO GO

Toronto is organized on a sensible grid pattern and possesses an excellent public transportation system, so it is easy to get around. On a map, note the main south–north arteries from west to east: Bathurst, Spadina, and University avenues, Bay, Yonge, Church, Jarvis, and Parliament streets. Yonge Street, the city's best known thoroughfare, is the central artery dividing west from east. It was constructed in 1795 as a military road leading 1,896km (1,173 miles) north to Rainy River in northern Ontario. The main east–west streets (going northward from Lake Ontario) are: Front, King, Queen, Dundas, College-Carlton, Wellesley and Bloor streets, with St Clair and Eglinton avenues farther north.

This sightseeing tour begins in one of the most attractive and active parts of the city, downtown on the lakeshore. We then make our way northward, with detours east and west, but you can easily devise your own tour to fit your schedule and interests. A useful first port of call is the Toronto Convention and Visitors Association offices in Queen's Quay Terminal at Harbourfront.

THE LAKESHORE

The city rises from the shores of Lake Ontario. Until the 1970s, the lakeshore was a wasteland of rotting piers, warehouses, and factories. Today, it's a superb 39-hectare (96-acre) urban waterfront park called **Harbourfront**, a playground filled with stores, cafés, theaters, galleries, and plenty of opportunities to get out on the water. Harbourfront hosts thousands of events during the year, including The Milk

A view of the mainland from the Islands

International Children's Festival and the International Festival of Authors, which features more than 60 authors from all over the world. In summer, cruises of the harbor and the islands leave from here on a variety of craft – glass-enclosed Amsterdam-style boats, paddle-wheelers, and three-masters – and there's also an outfit that rents canoes and kayaks. Take the romantic sunset cruise aboard the tall ship *The Challenge* and watch the lights of the city skyline appear on the horizon.

Harbourfront Centre

Start at **Queen's Quay West**, a warehouse that has been converted into a handsome shopping mall with a dance theater inside. Stroll along the waterfront to the building with a tall smokestack, the **Power Plant,** and check out what's showing in this contemporary art gallery. Behind it is the Enwave Theatre and behind that, **Harbourfront Centre** at 234 Queen's

The Harbourfront Centre art gallery

Quay West is the place to pick up information about Harbourfront events. Stop in at the craft studios and watch the artisans making glass, ceramics, jewelry, and metal sculptures. Kids enjoy the pool for model boats, and the winter ice rink, too.

Throughout June, July and August, Harbourfront Centre has themed mini-festivals at weekends, such

A potter at the craft studios

as the Latin Ritmos Y Color, the Caribbean Island Soul, the Ashkenaz Festival of Yiddish Culture and the international Hot & Spicy Food Festival. Each features a variety of exhibits, activities, food and entertainment. Performances on the outdoor stage near the water, where top local and international musical acts appear in concert are either free or modestly priced. Expect to catch artists such as Seu Jorge from Brazil, the Neville Brothers from the US, and Canada's Sarah Harmer at this venue.

Nearby, Harbourfront's International Marketplace runs all summer in a series of tents west of 234 Queen's Quay West. Here you'll find an assortment of quality but affordable crafts, clothing, jewelry and accessories from around the world.

The Pier

Cross the footbridge to **John Quay**, admiring the many vessels below as you go. Continue on to **Maple Leaf Quay**, where you can rent a canoe or kayak on the lake. Take a detour a few blocks north to King Street where you will find a local favorite, **Toronto Antiques on King** (276 King Street West; open Tue–Sun 10am–6pm). Here there are 100-plus

On the ferry to the Islands

dealers selling everything from sports equipment and military memorabilia to fantastic majolica, china, and silver. This is a frequent stop for visitors from Hollywood and other points south.

Head back to the quayside and at 95 Queen's Quay East you will find **Redpath Sugar Museum** (telephone ahead for hours, 416/933-8341). You can see the machinery and equipment involved in sugar production, and there are films on sugar harvesting and processing.

The Islands

The **Toronto Islands**, facing Harbourfront, are a favorite summer destination for Torontonians, who crowd the ferries with their bicycles and picnic hampers, headed for the shady paths and quiet waterways of the 14 islands. In 1858, a series of storms created the islands by shattering what was a peninsula joined to the Scarborough Bluffs east of the city center. Today, bridges link the islands so you can walk or cycle the length of them.

Ferries leave regularly in the summer from the docks behind the Westin Harbour Castle at the foot of Bay Street, calling at the three main islands. **Centre Island** is the most popular, but its beach and picnic areas can be crowded. Kids enjoy Centreville, an old-fashioned amusement park that includes a petting zoo. **Ward's Island** is favored by some for its lively boardwalk. (Between Centre and Ward's islands is the exclusive Royal Canadian Yacht Club, worth a visit if you belong to an affiliated organization or know a member.) **Hanlan's Point**, alongside Toronto Island Airport, has one of Toronto's only nude beaches along the western side. Due to pollution, Lake Ontario beaches are often closed to swimmers.

Ontario Place

Farther west along the lakeshore, you reach **Ontario Place**, a major summer attraction for visitors and Torontonians alike. Built on three man-made islands in 1971, this charming 39-hectare (96-acre) park is part Disneyland and part cultural center that has been cleverly integrated into the waterfront. The **Molson Amphitheatre** seats up to 16,000 people under a copper canopy and on the surrounding knoll, for evening classical, jazz and pop concerts. You can't miss the **Cinesphere** at the IMAX theater, 955 Lakeshore Road West. This white geodesic dome resembles a part-buried golf ball. Inside, on a curved screen six stories high, movies on subjects ranging from volcanic eruptions to earth and space exploration are screened regularly.

Ontario Place

Mounted on stilts, the **Atlantis Pavilions** contain a dance club, a video show, and the Atlantis Theatre. The **Children's Village** is imaginatively designed for youngsters aged 12 or under. There are some thrilling water rides, a series of duck ponds for toddlers to splash in, a large trampoline, and a children's theater. You can put your drenched kids through the huge 'dryer' shaped like a bird.

Across Lakeshore Boulevard, **Exhibition Place** hosts the annual Canadian National Exhibition during the end of August and early September, as well as other events throughout the year, such as the Royal Canadian Winter Fair.

Canada's Sports Hall of Fame (telephone ahead for hours 416/260-6789; free) is five minutes' walk away at the centre of Exhibition Park (just off Lakeshore Boulevard West). The two galleries have displays of great sporting events and players, but there are no references to the nation's most popular sport, hockey, which has its very own Hockey Hall of Fame downtown *(see page 38)*.

Farther west along the lakeshore lies **High Park**, which extends from the shore to Bloor Street. People come to this 162-hectare (400-acre) park to play cricket and baseball, and to picnic, cycle and jog. In winter they skate at the most atmospheric skating rink in the city, **Grenadier Pond**, where roasted chestnuts are sold from glowing braziers. There's also a small petting zoo, tennis courts, a swimming pool, and bowling greens. John G. Howard, who lived in **Colborne Lodge**, a charming English-style Regency cottage, donated the park to the city in 1873.

DOWNTOWN & FINANCIAL DISTRICT

Toronto started life as a strategic fort, and you can visit the original **Historic Fort York** just west of Bathurst behind the Gardiner Expressway. Originally the lake reached all the way up to the fort's circular battery. Built in 1793 by Lieutenant Governor John Graves Simcoe, it was

Seat of government

The Ontario Legislature sits on the site (some say appropriately) of a lunatic asylum.

The Toronto skyline at night

destroyed on 27 April 1813, when 2,700 American troops stormed ashore, drove out the British, and burned both the fort and the parliament buildings. See the authentically furnished l9th-century officer's quarters, historical displays, including a diorama of the Battle of York, and the Stone Magazine, where 900 barrels of gunpowder were stored. In summer it's fun to see the musket-firing drills performed by uniformed soldiers and hear the firing of the cannon at noon.

High Spot

For a quick geographical orientation, ride to the top of the **CN Tower** (301 Front Street West, tel: 416/868-6937; open Sun–Thur 9am–10pm, Fri–Sat 9am–10.30pm; admission fee), which pierces Toronto's sky like a gigantic hypodermic needle. At a bit more than 553m (1,815ft), it is one of the world's tallest free-standing structures, surpassed only by the Burj Dubai. Built between 1973 and 1975 by Canadian National

(CN), the government railroad and telecommunications company, the tower is a radio and television transmission mast, and a sure-fire tourist attraction. If your stomach drops away as the outdoor Plexiglas elevator rushes upward, consider that the speed of ascent is 6m (20ft) per second. First stop – 347m (1,128ft) up – is the **Sky Pod**, which has two observation decks. From this level you can see the entire city spread out below. To the south are the Toronto Islands, and facing them the waterfront and harbor, dotted with sails in summer. The futuristic complex to the west is Ontario Place (see page 31).

Another (indoor) elevator takes you up 33 more stories to the **Space Deck**, which at 447m (1,465ft) offers distant views – they say that on a clear day you can see all the way to Niagara Falls and Buffalo, New York state. If you're really daring, step on to the glass floor and look down.

Back down at the base, there are several virtual-reality and other cyber-games to entertain the whole family.

Baseball Attraction

Rogers Centre at 1 Blue Jays Way stands to the west of the tower. This giant stadium, seating 67,000, has become a tourist

Underground Toronto

It's not enough to know the name of surface streets in Toronto. In winter, it's wise to know how to negotiate the broad walkways that wind underground between buildings so you can avoid the freezing cold outside. You can, for example, walk all the way from the **Queen Street** subway station to Union Station, passing underneath the skyscrapers of the financial district. These well-signposted walkways are known as the PATH system. Branches lead off to the **Stock Exchange**, **Metro Hall**, and the **CBC Building**. A warren of similar underground walkways winds around **Bloor** and **Yonge** and elsewhere in the city.

attraction in itself, and admission is free when no events are on. It is one of the largest stadiums with a retractable roof, which covers 3 hectares (8 acres) and weighs 8.5 million kg (19 million lb). Amazingly, it only takes 750 horsepower (about six four-cylinder cars) and C$20 worth of electricity to close the four roof panels.

The Audience at Rogers Centre

Baseball fan or not, the tour is fascinating: you'll see the press-room accommodating 114 baseball reporters, the luxurious corporate boxes, and if you're lucky, the Clubhouse and locker rooms. On the exterior, look closely at *The Audience*, a sculpture of seven emotional fans by Michael Snow; Lutz Haufschild's glass sculpture *Tribute to Baseball* is above the southeast and southwest entrances.

Diagonally across Front Street, at 250 Front Street West, is the red and blue, box-like **CBC Building**, which is worth visiting to take a tour of the studios. Take some time to look in at the first-floor museum, which traces the development of CBC radio and TV, along with some interesting clips of shows and newsreels from times gone by.

Walk up John to King and you'll find **Metro Hall** (55 John Street), a seat of municipal government. Across the street, the **Princess of Wales Theatre** became a mecca for mourners when Princess Diana died in August 1997. The decorative murals painted by Frank Stella are worth a look inside. If you can't get in, check out the mural on the back of the building.

Farther east along King Street is the **Royal Alexandra Theatre**, an Edwardian treasure decked out in gobs of red velvet and gilt. This theater was saved by one of the city's most successful entrepreneurs, the prosperous Lithuanian immigrant ('Honest') Ed Mirvish, who began his career at Honest Ed's, a discount store on Bloor at Bathurst (in the 1970s he bought the Old Vic Theatre in London).

Diagonally opposite, at 60 Simcoe Street, is **Roy Thomson Hall**, named after the national newspaper proprietor Lord Thomson of Fleet, once owner of the London *Times*. Designed by Arthur Erickson, it has a mushroom-like exterior which looks particularly dramatic at night. One of the city's premier concert halls, it's home to the Toronto Symphony and stages many other musical events from around the world. After undergoing a C$24-million enhancement in 2002 to improve the acoustics (which are now top notch), the hall went on to win the Performing Arts Venue of the Year award in 2005. You can take a guided tour of the venue.

Rising skyscrapers

Financial Hub

Continue east along King and you'll come to the heart of the city's financial district. Skyscrapers rise on every side. At the northeast corner of University, the **Sun Life** building looms up behind sculptures by Sorel Etrog and Barbara Hepworth. Across York Avenue, you can visit the **Toronto Stock Exchange**, which opened in

1983, and learn about how the market works at the interactive displays in the visitor center.

On King between York and Bay stand two financial giants. On the north side of the street, **First Canadian Place** is home to the Bank of Montréal. On the south side rises the black glass tower of the **Toronto Dominion Centre**, designed by Mies

Sculpture outside Union Station

van der Rohe. The 36-floor IBM Tower, which is the third-highest of the four towers that make up the Centre, contains the **Toronto Dominion Gallery of Art Inuit Art** (open Mon–Fri 8am–6pm, Sat 10am–4pm; free), a fine collection of sculptures in stone, bone, antler and ivory. At the heart of the TD Centre is the somnolent sculpture *Pasture*, by Joe Fafard, of cows lounging on the grass. It's a reminder of the city's rural roots and of the source of its original wealth.

Cross Bay Street and pop into the **Canadian Imperial Bank** to see the impressive banking hall with coffered ceiling, carved gilded moldings, and sculpted friezes. In the early 1970s, the American architect I.M. Pei was asked to design a new complex around the building, creating the intimate **Commerce Court**.

At the foot of Bay Street in Front Street West stands **Union Station**, a grand neo-classical building with limestone columns and Italian tile ceilings. Built in 1927, it's still the city's main train station. Across the street, at 100 Front Street West, is the **Fairmont Royal York**, a hotel built on the site of the old Queen's Hotel by the Canadian Pacific Railway, and opened in 1929. For years it was Toronto's tallest

The Stanley Cup

building, and hosted every major city social event. The banquet rooms are still the most lavish in the city.

As you walk through the canyons of the Financial District you may glimpse sudden flashes of golden light. They are emanating from the incredible **Royal Bank Plaza** building, a pleated, gilded curtain at the corner of Front and Bay. Designed by Boris Zerafa, it is covered in 70kg (156lb) of real gold. Step inside, and you'll find a cathedral-high lobby and atrium decorated with thousands of aluminum cylinders, the work of Venezuelan sculptor Jesús Raphael Soto. Natural light shines on the ponds, waterfall, and lush greenery, making an inspiring experience.

On the other side of Bay Street, **BCE Place** is another remarkable building. The dramatic soaring galleria designed by the contemporary Spanish architect Santiago Calatrava was built around a beaux arts bank building that is now part of Toronto's **Hockey Hall of Fame** (30 Yonge Street; open Mon–Fri 10am–5pm, Sat 9.30am–6pm, Sun 10.30am–5pm; admission fee). This national shrine to the country's favorite sport contains the most comprehensive collection of hockey artifacts, displays, and memorabilia in the world.

Visitors can face down Mark Messier using a sponge puck, or practice shooting and keeping goal. You can see a replica of the Maple Leafs' dressing room, watch film clips that record great moments in the game, and ponder how people ever played with the early equipment on display. The coveted

Stanley Cup, the competition's most prestigious trophy, is displayed in front of the Honour Roll under the glorious dome of the rococo Bank of Montréal.

ST LAWRENCE MARKET AREA

On the east side of Yonge and Front, the **Hummingbird Centre**, a modern concrete building, has had to change its tune since the National Ballet of Canada and the Canadian Opera Company moved to their purpose-built home in 2006, the Four Seasons Centre for Performing Arts *(see page 42)*. However, it continues to program international dance, theater, children's shows and Christmas spectacles.

The **St Lawrence Centre for the Performing Arts** (27 Front Street East, tel: 416/366-7723) is home to the Canadian Stage Company. Sandwiched at the end of the park

Find fresh food at St Lawrence Market

The Flatiron building

between Front and Wellington is the **Gooderham**, or **Flatiron**, building (1892), built as the headquarters for George Gooderham, the largest distiller in the British Empire. The west facade sports an odd *trompe l'oeil* mural by Derek M. Besant.

A block away, at Jarvis and Front streets, the **St Lawrence Market** (open Tue–Sat) is a vast market hall where vendors sell super-fresh meats, fish, cheeses, and more. Try a Canadian back bacon sandwich here. Saturdays are particularly lively when there is a farmer's market and street entertainment as well.

Nearby on King Street, the Palladian-style **St Lawrence Hall** with its domed cupola (1851) was the focal point of city life in the 19th century. Frederick Douglass spoke here, Jenny Lind and Adelina Patti sang here, and just about everyone, from General Tom Thumb to Buffalo Bill, appeared here.

Across King Street, the steeple of the Anglican **St James Cathedral** soars into the sky. John Strachan (later a bishop) was its most famous incumbent, a fierce Anglophile who threatened the Americans with the British Navy when they sacked York (Toronto), and who dismissed Thomas Jefferson as a mischief-maker. The building was begun in 1850 and completed in 1874. Inside is a Tiffany stained-glass window.

At 115 King, the **Toronto Sculpture Garden** is a serene corner for a bit of rest. At Church and King streets, the **King Edward Hotel** is the city's oldest such establishment and much beloved by well-heeled Torontonians for its high-tea service.

DOWNTOWN WEST

If you walk up Bay from King Street, past the venerable department store HBC (shortened from Hudson's Bay Company), you'll have a marvelous view of **Old City Hall**, a magnificent Romanesque Revival building designed by Edward James Lennox in 1885. The carved heads on the pillars that support the portico include famous political figures of the period and a portrait of the architect himself. Today it houses the Provincial Criminal Courts. It's worth going inside to see the striking stained-glass window by Robert McCausland.

To the west across Bay Street rise the two semicircular towers flanking a saucer-shaped building which make up new **City Hall**, designed by Finnish architect Viljo Revell and completed in 1965. Henry Moore's statue *The Archer* stands out

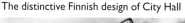

The distinctive Finnish design of City Hall

front in Nathan Phillips Square, where Torontonians gather in summer and skate in winter. Inside are some engaging art works; at the entrance is David Partridge's *Metropolis*, created from more than 100,000 nails. You can also sit in on the proceedings in the circular council chamber. In the southwest corner of the square, you might encounter someone railing about some topic to the interest or derision of anyone seated nearby, for this is Toronto's own Speaker's Corner, watched over by a stern statue of Winston Churchill.

West along Queen Street, **Osgoode Hall** is a lovely golden stone-and-brick Georgian building that is the seat of the Law Society of Upper Canada which you can visit on a tour. The central building contains a magnificent library.

Campbell House (160 Queen Street West; open Mon–Fri 9.30am–4.30pm; admission fee) on the northwest corner of Queen and University, is an exemplary red-brick Georgian mansion you can tour that once belonged to Sir William Campbell, Chief Justice of Upper Canada. In 1972, the house was moved here from its original site about 3km (2 miles) away.

At the southeast corner of Queen and University is the sparkling glass façade of **The Four Seasons Centre for the Performing Arts**, which opened in 2006 as home to the Canadian Opera Company and National Ballet. The building has the longest free-spanning glass staircase in the world.

Boutiques galore

Funky Shopping

From John Street to Dovercourt Road, **Queen Street West** offers a long, diverse stretch of eclectic shops. The city's funkiest shopping street, it has a melange of antiques and retro stores, design shops, antiquarian bookstores, up-and-coming fashion designer boutiques, and other cutting-edge emporiums. West on this stretch is a growing art gallery district, specifically between Ossington and Gladstone. Artist Katherine Mulherin pioneered the strip with galleries at 1040, 1080 and 1086 Queen Street West. Stephen Bulger's elegant photography gallery is at 1026; others include [Bracket] Gallery at 1168, featuring vernacular arts and, beyond the railway underpass at 1338 is Made You Look, a co-op jewelry studio and gallery.

Eaton Centre, where all but the Eatons prosper

Reserve a space on the tour at CHUMCity, the city's advanced TV station where everything is on wheels and ready to go at a moment's notice. It also operates MuchMusic, a channel similar to MTV, and an arts channel.

North of Queen Street at Dundas and Yonge streets, the **Eaton Centre** (open Mon–Fri 10am–9pm, Sat 9.30am–7pm, Sun noon–6pm) is where the average Torontonian shops. Anchored at both ends by skyscrapers, it opens into a 264-m (866-ft) glass galleria dotted with benches, palm trees, and fountains, and graced by Michael Snow's *Flight Stop*, a cluster of 60 soaring Canada geese. Eb Zeidler, who also designed Ontario Place, designed the center in 1975.

Originally, it was a monument to the merchandising Eaton family, who for more than a century followed the motto 'Goods Satisfactory or Money Refunded.' Eaton's declared bankruptcy in the 1990s, but the current owners of the mall retain the prestigious name.

Holy Trinity Church, huddled in the shadow of the Eaton Centre, was saved from destruction because Torontonians wanted it so. The Gothic Revival structure is one of the city's oldest buildings (1847), along with its neighbor, the Scadding House which was formerly the pastor's residence. It's hard to believe that the church's towers were once used as navigational landmarks for approaching sailing vessels. The church is an important venue for artistic events and is well known for its excellent acoustics.

On Bond Street, two blocks east of Yonge and just south of Dundas, the Victorian **Mackenzie House** (tel: 416/392-6915, call for hours; admission fee) was built for Toronto's first mayor, William Lyon Mackenzie. A firebrand reformer who led a revolt in 1837 *(see page 19)*, he was exiled but later returned to Toronto, living here until his death in 1861. The interior has been impeccably restored; you can see the hand-operated flatbed printing press he used for his revolutionary newspaper, the *Colonial Advocate*.

Allan Gardens Conservatory (19 Horticultural Avenue, tel: 416/392-7288; open daily 10am–5pm; free) is on Gerrard Street east of Jarvis. The spectacular glass-domed Palm House is modeled on the one at Kew in Britain. The area is rather seedy and should be avoided at night.

Tucked away on Centre Avenue just off Dundas West is the **Textile Museum of Canada** (open Tue, Thur, Fri 11am–5pm, Wed 11am–8pm, Sat–Sun noon–5pm; admission fee), which has a large collection of ultra-fine textiles from all over the world. Temporary exhibitions showcase traditional textile crafts alongside contemporary fabric art.

Centre for Art

West along Dundas Street, the **Art Gallery of Ontario** (call 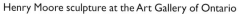 for hours 416/979-6648; admission fee) is heralded by *Large Two Forms* by the British sculptor Henry Moore (1898–1986) at the corner of McCaul Street. The gallery re-opened in fall 2008 after a massive expansion designed by lauded architect Frank Gehry, who was raised in Toronto. Five thousand artworks have been re-installed in 110 galleries. Inside the Henry Moore Sculpture Centre there are 800 of the artist's works, including original plasters, bronzes, woodcuts, lithographs, and drawings. Moore himself designed the main gallery, using natural light to enhance the monumental casts used for many of his celebrated bronzes.

The Canadian galleries feature the Group of Seven *(see page 46)*. Look for *Above Lake Superior* by Lawren Harris, which is representative of the Group's landscape style.

Henry Moore sculpture at the Art Gallery of Ontario

Other galleries feature historic works by such early Canadian painters as Paul Kane and Cornelius Krieghoff, who recorded frontier life, and Homer Watson, dubbed 'Canada's Constable'. More modern Canadians include Paul-Emile Borduas, William Ronald, Kazuo Nakamura, Harold Town, and Jack Bush, all members of Toronto's Painters Eleven, a modern, mostly abstract group, which flourished from 1953 to 1960. Also, essential for art lovers are the Inuit galleries. The European collections are also strong, with the beautiful and funny series of proverbs painted by Brueghel the Younger.

The gallery is built around **The Grange** (call for information 416/979-6648; admission fee), an elegant Georgian coun-

The Group of Seven

The Group of Seven painters revolutionized Canadian landscape painting in the first half of the 20th century, and put Canadian painting on the international art map. The original 'seven' consisted of **Franklin Carmichael**, **Lawren Harris**, **A.Y. Jackson**, **Frank Johnston**, **Arthur Lismer**, **J.E.H. MacDonald**, and **Frederick Varley**. Before World War I, several of them had worked with and been inspired by **Tom Thomson**, who had quit commercial art to paint Canadian landscapes; after he drowned in 1917, his followers continued what he had begun.

The Group of Seven were criticized for turning away from the then-current slavish imitation of European styles, deriving inspiration instead first from Toronto, then from the harsh and beautiful landscape of Northern Ontario. These artists painted rocks, pines, snow, and water in the open air, sometimes so schematically that they appeared as abstracts. This can be seen most clearly in the work of Lawren Harris. The group added members and also influenced others, including **Emily Carr**. They went on to paint scenes in the Rocky Mountains, the west coast, and the Arctic Circle. The Group disbanded in 1932, but the Canadian landscape-painting movement survived into the 1950s.

try house built in 1817 by D'Arcy Boulton, Jr, a member of the ruling elite, on an estate that once stretched 3½km (2 miles) from Queen Street up to Bloor Street. His son's widow married journalist and Oxford Professor of Modern History Goldwin Smith, who entertained lavishly. Today, the Grange represents upper-class life in 1840. Note the circular cantilevered staircase and stained-glass windows. From here you can see the colorful, cantilevered addition to the Ontario College of Art and Design, by British architect Will Alsop.

Chinatown

Chinatown

As you go farther west along Dundas, the ambience becomes progressively Asian. Toronto's **Chinatown** developed around Dundas and Elizabeth streets, but high-rises, parking garages, and the new City Hall forced it west along Dundas and north up Spadina Avenue. Today, Toronto has several Chinatowns out in the suburbs. Dundas is as much Vietnamese as Chinese, but you'll still find supermarkets and groceries selling exotic vegetables and fish, tea vendors, bakeries, restaurants, herbal medicine shops, and other entrepôts selling everything from Asian music to paper lanterns.

From Dundas turn onto Kensington Avenue to visit **Kensington Market**, once the heart of the Jewish community and later of the Portuguese community. Now more Caribbean in flavor, traces of its earlier days are still in evidence: stores selling yucca and all kinds of peppers, fish stores selling *bacalhau*, dairies selling cheeses and sour cream, vendors with racks of vintage clothes, plus dried goods stores selling beans, rice, and dried fruits. The neighborhood has retained its character as an outdoor market and it is also a good place to stop for a coffee or to try an empañada (a stuffed pastry).

QUEEN'S PARK & UNIVERSITY AREA

At College Street, University Avenue suddenly opens into oval-shaped **Queen's Park** with, at its center, the pink sandstone **Provincial Parliament Buildings**. On a tour, you can sit in on question time at 2pm, or listen to one of the screaming matches that pass for debates in the provincial chamber.

The Parliament Building

On the southwestern side of the park, the curved, mirrored building that catches the eye is the **Ontario Hydro** building, housing the offices of the water and electricity board. It sets an ecological example, as it is lit and heated from underground thermal reservoirs.

West of Queen's Park between College and Bloor, the **University of Toronto** is considered by many to be Canada's premier university.

Among its famous alumni are Frederick Banting and Charles Best, who discovered insulin here in 1921. From College Street, turn up King's College Road to visit some of the architectural and cultural highlights on the campus. Look across the playing fields of King's College Circle to University College, a fabulous Romanesque Revival building dating from 1859. Because it was nonsectarian,

Graduation day, University of Toronto

it was once called the Godless College. Around the corner, **Hart House** is the most Gothic-looking Oxford-style building on the campus. Go in to see the small chapel, the common rooms, and the impressive Great Hall with its hammer-beam ceiling, stained glass, and massive fireplace.

Hart House also has a theater and the **Justina M. Barnicke Art Gallery** (open Mon–Fri 11am–7pm, Sat–Sun 1–4pm; free), with a fine collection of Canadian art. Soldier's Memorial Tower, inspired by the bell tower of Magdalen College in Oxford, Britain, stands between Hart House and University College. It houses a full carillon, which is played regularly. Exit to Hoskin Avenue and you'll see one of the most controversial modern buildings on campus – the **Robarts Library**, the universty's main humanities and social sciences library. The brutal concrete structure is said by some to resemble a giant peacock, but students commonly refer to it as the Turkey. East along Hoskin is another modern building, Massey College (1960–1963), designed by architect Ron Thom, around a quad with playing fountain. For many years the writer Robertson Davies was the master of the college.

Canadian hero

Superman is not American. He was invented by Torontonian Joe Shuster.

North of the University area is **The Annex** (Avenue Road to Bathurst Street, Bloor Street to Dupont Street), a residential area largely populated by academics living in handsome Victorian homes. In keeping with its cultural aspirations, the district has a good share of restaurants, cafés and craft boutiques, plus a movie theater.

BLOOR-YORKVILLE AREA

This is the city's high-end shopping district, and also the location of several of its top-rated museums.

At Bloor and St George, the **Bata Shoe Museum** (open Tue–Sat 10am–5pm, Thur 10am–8pm, Sun noon–5pm; admission fee), located in a striking modern building designed by Raymond Moriyama, is unique. The core collection tells the story of footwear, beginning with the first human footprints discovered in Africa by anthropologist Mary Leakey, and examines the role that it has played ever since as status symbol, fashion statement, and tool. Some amazing specimens of the status-symbol variety are on display, such as the 18th-century, Italian, high-heeled coral shoes with silver thread embroidery and silver-and-paste buckles. Part of the show focuses on shoes used in rites of passage – bridal and funerary footwear, for example.

The most fascinating are the shoes devised for special functions, such as the 19th-century spiked French chestnut crushers or the outrageous plate-shaped American clown shoes. Designer shoes from Ferragamo, Henry Rayne, and Manolo Blahnik are included too, and the whole show finishes with State Turns, a collection of shoes that have been worn by the famous – the singer Elton John's 12-inch silver platforms, pianist Glenn Gould's battered black Oxfords, and prime minister of India Indira Gandhi's sturdy plain black pumps.

Royal Ontario Museum

Around the corner on Queen's Park, is the **Royal Ontario Museum** (known as the ROM; open Mon–Thur 10am–5.30pm, Fri 10am–9.30pm, Sat and Sun 10am–5.30pm; admission fee). The ROM is undergoing a massive transformation and expansion of its exhibition space designed by Daniel Libeskind, whose designs for the Jewish Museum in Berlin and the World Trade Center in New York have garnered him international acclaim. At the north side of the museum building are elaborate crystal-inspired prisms, the Michael Lee-Chin Crystal, unveiled in 2007. It houses the main entrance and seven galleries. Work will continue until 2010. Originally opened in 1912, the museum has a renowned Chinese collection, a superb Canadian decorative arts department, and some exciting life-science galleries.

George Crofts, a fur trader and entrepreneur who lived in Tianjin, China, gathered much of the brilliant Chinese collection; after he died in 1925 the Anglican bishop of Hunan, William Charles White, continued adding to it. The collection

Palaeontology in the Royal Ontario Museum

includes outstanding Buddhist wall paintings and monumental sculptures, an amazing procession of earthenware figures dating from the sixth and seventh centuries, plus portions of a Ming tomb. There are also beautiful snuffboxes, jade pieces, bronze vessels, china, and furniture.

The Egyptian galleries contain several mummies, including those of animals; the Roman collection is the best in Canada, while the Sigmund Samuel Canadiana galleries have rich and elaborate room settings, revealing the contribution that both French- and English-trained artisans made to Canadian culture.

Hollywood North

Third after Los Angeles and New York, Toronto is one of the largest film and television production centers in North America and the second largest exporter of television programming. On any given day, there are between 18 and 45 productions shooting in Toronto. This includes feature films, made-for-TV movies, and television shows (not including commercials and music videos). Toronto's Film and Television Office issues over 4,000 permits a year, giving around 1,200 projects permission to shoot on location and Torontonians have had to get used to the disruption caused by filming in almost every corner of their city. *The Hurricane, Good Will Hunting,* and *Chicago* are among the hundreds of movies shot in Toronto in the past few years.

State-of-the-art facilities, services from pre-production to post-production, a diversity of locations, and skilled labor have made the city a producer's paradise. Celebrities often remark that they can work in Toronto with relative anonymity.

For 10 days every September, journalists, distributors, directors, and actors mill around various Toronto theaters to attend press and industry screenings. This is the **Toronto International Film Festival**, the largest and most anticipated event on the movie community's fall calendar.

Among the life science galleries, the dinosaur skeletons are displayed against re-creations of their natural habitats. There is also the Bat Cave, where 3,000 lifelike bats congregate in a cave modeled on the St Clair cave in Jamaica.

Ceramics Museum

Across the street from the ROM, is the **Gardiner Museum of Ceramic Art** (open daily from 10am; admission fee; Fri free 4–9pm). The museum was founded on a magnificent ceramics collection assembled by businessman and financier George Gardiner in 1984, and has now expanded to include works from all over the world dating from 3500 BC to the present day. The pre-Columbian displays are exemplary, with superb Olmec and Maya figures, utensils, and objects. Other galleries have dazzling displays of Italian majolica from Faenza, Florence, and Venice. There's also a fine collection of Delftware. The European porcelain galleries contain numerous treasures – fine examples of Meissen, Sèvres, Chelsea, Bow, Royal Worcester, Derby, and much more. The Swan Service made by Meissen in the 18th century, consisting of 2,200 pieces, is remarkable. The museum shop is considered to be one of the best in town and celebrity chef, Jamie Kennedy, runs the restaurant.

Head by Jean-Pierre Larocque

Yorkville

North of Bloor between Avenue Road and Yonge Street, **Yorkville** is a great neighborhood for strolling, filled as it is with boutiques, galleries, and cafés. In the 1960s and early 1970s it was a hippie hangout, but now it is the most fashionable shopping district in Toronto. Hazelton Lanes is the most exclusive mall within the area. Along the way there are several architectural highlights to admire.

The **Toronto Reference Library**, a massive red-brick and glass building designed by Raymond Moriyama – who also masterminded the Ontario Science Centre – stands at the corner of Yonge between Cumberland and Yorkville avenues. The Library's interior is breathtaking: a light-filled atrium several stories high, accented with luxuriant vegetation as well as a fountain and pond. A Plexiglas elevator travels between floors.

NORTH OF BLOOR

Casa Loma

North of The Annex at 1 Austin Terrace is **Casa Loma** (open daily 9.30am–5pm; admission fee), which is something of a curiosity. Some call it a marvel, others a neo-Gothic monstrosity; whatever you may think, you certainly won't deny it's impressive. Fascinated by medieval castles, financier Sir Henry Pellatt built the 98-room mansion between 1905 and 1911 for C$3.5 million. He assembled materials from all over the world: oak and walnut from North America; teak from Asia; and the paneling, marble, and glass from several European countries. Labor too was imported, including Scottish stonemasons, who built the huge wall around the 2-hectare (5-acre) grounds.

Pellatt's sense of the grandiose can be seen in the paneled Oak Room (which took European artisans three years to complete) and the stained-glass dome, marble floors, and Italianate bronze doors of the Conservatory. Peacock Alley, a hall with carved oak walls, takes its name and shape from one in Windsor Castle. An 800-m (2,500-ft) tunnel runs from the wine cellar to the stables, where the horses were royally housed in a setting of Spanish tile and mahogany. You can also follow the financier's secret escape route – a hidden staircase leading from his study.

Spadina

Almost next door **Spadina Historic House and Gardens** (open Tue–Sun noon–5pm; admission fee) is a less fantastical mansion built by another financier, James Austin. It contains some rich collections assembled by the Austin family, who occupied the house, with its beautiful 2½-hectare (6-acre) garden, from 1866 to 1980.

Casa Loma, the quirkiest house in Toronto

Cemeteries

And where do socially prominent Torontonians lie in state? At **Mount Pleasant Cemetery** in Rosedale, where you can find mausoleums belonging to the Massey and Eaton families as well as the graves of such famous people as Glenn Gould, Prime Minister Mackenzie King, and Drs Banting and Best.

The beautiful **Necropolis**, in secluded Cabbagetown, also has some famous remains, notably William Lyon Mackenzie, leader of the 1837 rebellion, Lount and Matthews, the men who were hanged for treason, and famous oarsman Ned Hanlan. Note the charming chapel and the carriage entrance to the cemetery.

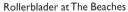

Rollerblader at The Beaches

SATELLITE NEIGHBORHOODS

The real Toronto is found in its many distinct **neighborhoods**, that are clustered around Downtown. Yorkville, Chinatown, and Kensington have already been mentioned, but there are others only short rides east or west by streetcar.

The Beaches lies at the eastern end of Queen Street. It's a residential district occupied largely by young professionals and their families who appreciate the long boardwalk and the recreational facilities on the waterfront.

Ethnic Areas

East of Jarvis Street, toward the Don River between Carlton and Wellesley, **Cabbagetown** is the memorable name given to an area once described as the 'largest Anglo-Saxon slum in North America.' Some say it was called Cabbagetown because people planted cabbages in their yards. It's been gentrified, although there are still some derelict buildings. Now the handsome Victorian residences are home to artists, actors, and other professionals. The **Wellesley Cottages** in this neighborhood have been credited as being one of the only indigenous forms of Ontario architecture. Cabbagetown's **Riverdale Farm** is a bucolic tract of land amid the urban sprawl, where passersby can watch farm hands milk goats and make cheese.

Across the Don River on Danforth Avenue (the eastward continuation of Bloor Street), **Greektown** is as Greek as Athens' own Plaka, with dozens of restaurants, bakeries, and other stores that cater to the Greek community.

North and east of Bloor stretches the city's most elite neighborhood, **Rosedale**, where those endowed with Toronto's 'old money' live in grand homes on tree-lined streets. Second on the totem pole, west of Avenue Road between St Clair and Eglinton, **Forest Hill** is home to the exclusive Upper Canada College and Bishop Strachan School for Girls.

Markham Village, on Markham Street west of Bathurst, is a block-long street of antiques shops, bookstores, art galleries, and restaurants, housed in Victorian buildings restored by mogul Ed Mirvish and his son David. Honest Ed's, on Bloor, is a curiosity of a discount store, opened by Mirvish soon after he arrived from Lithuania.

Saris and silks

Little India stretches from Coxwell to Greenwood Avenue on Gerrard. Here you'll find stores with colorful saris and silks, and many others selling Indian music and, of course, spices and herbs.

Behind the gaudiness and the punning signs – 'Only the floors are crooked!' – there are some good buys here.

Little Italy stretches along College Street between Euclid and Shaw. This strip has one of the liveliest patio scenes in the summer months. A second Italian neighborhood called the Corso Italia is found northwest of Casa Loma, along St Clair Avenue West between Lansdowne and Westmount Avenue.

Little Poland refers to a stretch of Roncesvalles Avenue between King and Dundas, where you'll find businesses catering to the East European and Russian community.

Portugal Village is bordered by College, Spadina, Ossington, and Trinity Bellwoods Park. Here you'll find fish markets, *churrasqueiras*, bakeries, cheese stores, and more, particularly along College and Dundas.

Koreatown extends along Bloor Street West between Bathurst and Christie. All are great places for ethnic food.

The high-tech Ontario Science Centre

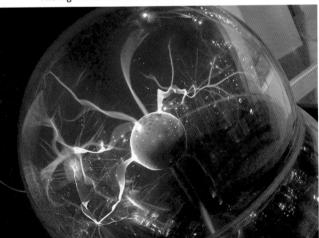

THE OUTSKIRTS

Ontario Science Centre

Just 10km (7 miles) northeast of Downtown, the **Ontario Science Centre** (770 Don Mills Road at Eglinton Avenue East; open daily 10am–5pm; admission fee) nestles in a ravine on the Don River Valley. With hundreds of hands-on exhibits in large exhibit halls, the Centre is a dazzling, high-tech palace of marvels, which was transformed by a multimillion dollar renovation completed in 2006. Everyone is so eager to play the scientific games that they hardly notice the fabulous building designed by Raymond Moriyama.

All the sciences have their place here, from anatomy to zoology, and you can learn all sorts of things by just standing around and looking. But what makes it such fun are all the interactive displays and the demonstrations. You can make your hair stand on end by touching 500,000 volts and see sparks fly 50cm (almost 20in). You can talk to a computer; see a laser burn through a brick; generate enough energy to lift a balloon; photograph yourself in the dark with a heat-sensitive camera; whisper anything but secrets into the parabolic sound reflectors and hear it broadcast across a room. The Omnimax Theatre, with a 24-m (79-ft) domed screen, shows a series of special-effects movies.

Important tips: go early, and try to avoid weekends, because the Science Centre attracts millions of visitors every year.

The Zoo

An hour's drive northeast of Downtown via Highway 401 and Meadowvale Road is the **Toronto Zoo** (361a Old Finch Avenue, Scarborough; open summer 9am–7.30pm, winter 9.30am–4.30pm; admission fee). Modeled on the famous San Diego zoo, it covers 287 hectares (710 acres), on which more than 5,000 animals are housed either in pavilions encapsulating complete natural habitats or outside in spacious paddocks. Colored walkways trace easy routes through the park (take blue for a fairly quick walking tour of major pavilions in all weather). Or you can take the Domain Tram, which operates year-round; in summer, the Zoomobile allows you to get on and off at the stops you choose.

The pavilions represent major zoological areas of the world: Africa, Indo-Malaysia, the Americas, Eurasia, and Australasia. They each contain the fauna and flora typical of the region, so visitors will find Florida alligators slithering in the swamps, Canadian beavers grinding their teeth in ponds, and Malaysian orangutans grooming themselves in the jungle. The Africa Savannah Project re-creates the African veldt with rhinos, hippos, giraffes, cheetahs, and lions. Littlefootland brings children into close contact with the more approachable animals, and audiovisual aids help to increase individual participation in the 'animal geography' experience.

A visit to the zoo can make for a long day, so remember to take advantage of the picnic tables at the rest stops.

Pioneer Village

Re-creating the 19th century

Black Creek Pioneer Village (1000 Murray Ross Parkway – Downsview at Steeles Avenue and Jane Street; open May–June Mon–Fri 9.30am–4pm, Sat–Sun 11am–5pm, Oct–Dec Mon–Fri 9.30am–4pm, Sat–Sun 11am–4.30pm, July–Sept Mon–Fri 10am–5pm, Sat–Sun 11am–5pm; admission fee), a step back in time to 19th-century Ontario, is a 40-minute drive north-west of Downtown.

More than 35 restored homes, workshops, public buildings and farms re-create the atmosphere of life in a rural Victorian community of the 1860s. Costumed guides demonstrate rural pursuits: tilling the land, grinding flour in the mill, making barrels, weaving textiles, and forging iron. You can stop for lunch in the country Post House Inn. Horse-drawn carts or sleighs haul happy children around the large property, and throughout the year there are parties for harvesting, sheep shearing, and other seasonal pursuits.

Black Creek Pioneer Village

Theme Park

Near the village is **Canada's Wonderland** (9580 Jane Street, Vaughn – off Highway 400 at Rutherford Road; open Sept and May Sat–Sun 10am–8pm, June daily 10am–8pm, July–Aug daily 10am–10pm). This 120-hectare (300-acre) Disney-style park has 200 attractions, including 15 roller coasters, a go-kart track, and Splashworks, an 8-hectare (20-acre) water park with 16 water-slides and a huge wave pool that generates whitecaps. Two theaters provide entertainment, while *Star Trek* and Hanna Barbera characters make appearances on the street. Batting cages and other sports facilities round out the complex.

Canadian Collection

Just up the road on the outskirts of the village of Kleinburg is the **McMichael Canadian Art Collection** (10365 Islington Avenue, tel: 905/893-1121; open daily 10am–4pm; admission fee). Work by the artists known as the Group of Seven is displayed in the former home of collectors Robert and Signe McMichael, a building constructed from native stone and timber in a beautiful forest setting. By 1964, the owners had accumulated so much art that they decided to allow the public to view their private collection; a museum was built (with state help) adjacent to the original house, and in the same style.

Polar Bear by Paula Saila at the McMichael Canadian Collection

The McMichaels still take a keen interest in the collection and, indeed, there has been a long-running battle fought between the current curators and the family about the present and future direction of the museum. The works of each of the Group of Seven *(see page 46)*, plus such figures as Emily Carr, J.W. Beatty, and Charles Comfort are hung together so that the individual development of each can be easily traced.

Several galleries are also devoted to First Nation artists such as Norval Morrisseau, Daphne Odjig, and Alex Janvier, and there are some fine Inuit soapstone sculptures on display.

OTHER NEARBY ATTRACTIONS

In Mississauga southwest of the city, **Playdium** (tel: 905/273-4810) on Rathburn Road offers 40,000 square feet of the latest in interactive pleasures. It has more than 260 games and simulators. If that's not enough, there are such other entertainments as climbing walls, a go-kart track, an IMAX theater, and batting cages. Surreal indeed.

In Burlington off Queen Elizabeth Way about 64km (40 miles) outside Toronto, you can visit the 1,000-hectare (2,500-acre) **Royal Botanical Gardens** (680 Plains Road West, Burlington, tel: 905/527 1158; open daily 10am until dusk; admission fee), the largest botanical gardens in Canada.

The gardens offer superb, colorful displays of lilac, magnolia, rhododendron, and azalea in spring, plus a host of bearded iris and peonies a little later in June. There's a spectacular rose garden with 3,000 plants, plus a rock garden, annual and perennial gardens, scent and medicinal gardens, 1,120 varieties of hedge plant, an arboretum and the RBG Centre (conservatory) with its year-round display. A double-decker bus provides a free shuttle service; walkers will appreciate the 50km (31 miles) of trails, many leading to the wetlands where heron and other bright water birds can be seen.

EXCURSIONS FROM TORONTO

Niagara Falls is only 128km (80 miles) from Toronto. En route you might want to stop in Hamilton to visit **Dundurn Castle** (610 York Boulevard; open July–Sept daily 10am–4pm, Oct–June Tue–Sun noon–4pm; admission fee). Sir Allan Napier MacNab, a lawyer, industrialist, politician, and joint premier of the United Province of Canada from 1854–56, built this neoclassical mansion. MacNab went bankrupt, but the house has been restored to its former splendor.

Niagara Falls

In spite of honeymooners' hype and over-commercialization, **Niagara Falls** are still far too awesome to be shrugged off as a tourist trap. The 129 million liters (34 million gallons) of water a minute roaring over those limestone cliffs, and the rising white mist, make the most jaded tourists stop and stare.

The first European to record seeing the falls was a French priest, Father Louis Hennepin, in December 1678. He reckoned that the escarpment was 92m (302ft) high, when in fact it is only 51m (167ft) high. Given the breathtaking sight, it's not surprising that he overestimated the drop.

Niagara Falls became a honeymoon capital supposedly after Napoleon's brother arrived with his bride by stagecoach from New Orleans. Rapt young couples still come, posing in front of the falls for that memorable photograph.

The **American Falls**, facing you as you stand on the Canadian side, are 300m (1,076ft) wide; the more spectacular Canadian **Horseshoe Falls**, named for their shape, are nearly 800m (2,600ft) wide. The two are separated by tiny **Goat Island**, which was named for its original inhabitants.

You can view the falls from above, beside, or beneath. From **Rainbow Bridge**, which crosses to the US, walk along for a couple of kilometers in the **Queen Victoria Park** area, viewing the American

Maid of the Mist sails to Niagara Falls

Falls opposite, and stop at Table Rock House, perched facing the brink of Horseshoe Falls. Lifts descend to scenic tunnels with portals for viewing the mighty waters from below. Don the raincoat that's offered, it's very wet down there. Around **Table Rock House** are stores and restaurants, as well as many walkways and viewpoints.

The ***Maid of the Mist*** (tel: 905/358-5781; several sailings daily May–Oct) is a famous boat, named for a legendary First Nation girl who was given to the falls as 'bride of the river.' The exciting 30-minute boat trip up to the booming waters is both deafening and drenching; rain-slickers are offered with the ride.

Several towers afford bird's-eye views, including the **Minolta**, at 190m (575ft), and the **Skylon**, at 258m (775ft), both of which have other attractions, such as an aquarium, a glass museum, a revolving restaurant, amusement rides, and snack bars. The **Clifton Hill** area offers several so-called museums – waxworks, the **Guinness Museum of World Records**, and **Ripley's Believe It or Not! Museum**. On River Road, the **Niagara Falls Museum** has a melange of First Nation artifacts and nature exhibits. There are also two casinos, the sprawling **Casino Niagara** and the **Fallsview Casino**.

Farther along River Rapids Road, the **Great Gorge Trip** takes you down by elevator to view the turbulent rapids and see the **Daredevil Exhibit**, which pays tribute to the crazies who made it alive, or dead, over the falls in various conveyances, mostly barrels. One section is devoted to the French tightrope walker Blondin, who made regular trips across the falls on a wire during 1859 and 1860.

Under the Falls

From Whirl-a-Port, at Victoria Avenue and Niagara Parkway, you can take a **helicopter flight** for an exhilarating overview of the falls. On the Niagara River, the foaming Whirlpool can be seen from a cable car, called the **Spanish Aero Car**, as it swings 549m (1,800ft) up over the gorge.

The Canadian side of the falls has been beautifully landscaped. The **Niagara Parkway**, which runs 56km (35 miles) along the Niagara River, is lined with bucolic picnic areas, fruit farms, gardens, and parks. Highlights along the way include the **Niagara Parks Botanical Gardens and School of Horticulture**, where the gardens offer seasonal displays, plus the famous **Floral Clock**, which has 25,000 plants within a diameter of 40m (131ft). **The Butterfly Conservatory** is a delightful place where more than 2,000 butterflies dance and flutter among the nectar-producing plants.

Other interesting stopping places include the Georgian-style **McFarland House** (open May–Sept; admission fee) and the **Laura Secord House** (open May–Oct; admission fee), which belonged to a courageous Loyalist who warned the British troops of an imminent American invasion during the War of 1812. You will also pass **Fort George**, which was the main British outpost on the Niagara frontier during the War of 1812. It was leveled by American artillery in 1813 and gradually reconstructed since 1930, and is today manned by 'soldiers' in British uniform, who demonstrate 19th-century military drills. From here, the parkway leads into Niagara-on-the-Lake.

Niagara-on-the-Lake

This 19th-century historic town, the first capital of Upper Canada, has been restored with some style. It is famous for the **Shaw Festival** (April–Nov; <www.shawfest.com>) which started in 1962 to celebrate the works of the Irish playwright

---

Energy source

Half of the 129 million liters (34 million gallons) of water that pour over the edge of Niagara Falls every minute is now diverted by the US and Canada for electric power, making it the largest producer of hydro-electricity in the world.

George Bernard Shaw (1856–1950). It is now one of the largest repertory companies in North America, with performances given by outstanding Canadian and British casts. Works by Shaw's contemporaries are also staged.

There are three theaters in town, but the main **Festival Theatre** at Wellington Street and Queen's Parade Road, on the edge of town, is worth a visit even if you don't attend a performance. A handsome contemporary brick-and-glass structure with a wonderful native wood interior, it also has an attractive garden with willow trees and a pond – a perfect setting for intermission drinks.

Shaded Queen Street leads past **Simcoe Park**, a favorite place for picnics, and on the opposite side of the street, past the Prince of Wales Hotel. A stroll along Queen Street will take you past clapboard and brick buildings occupied by boutiques, cafés, ice-cream parlors, and other emporiums.

A vineyard in Niagara wine country

The **Welland Canal** cuts through the Niagara Escarpment. It was built to circumvent Niagara Falls and connect lower-lying Lake Ontario to Lake Erie, which is about 100m (327ft) higher. The first canal was built in 1829, making it possible for deep-ocean-going vessels to navigate through the Great Lakes into the interior. This engineering feat – 42km (26 miles) long and 8m (27ft) deep – has seven locks along it, each with an average lift of 14m (47ft). It's amazing to watch the locks function. There's a viewing station at Lock 3 in St Catherine's and at Lock 8 in Port Dalhousie. For visitor information tel: 905/688-6462.

Niagara Wine Country

The Niagara Peninsula is home to more than 30 wineries, most of which offer tours and tastings. From Niagara-on-the-Lake take Highway 55 (Niagara Stone Road) to the **Hillebrand Estates Winery**, outside Virgil, which offers tours, wine tasting, and special events during summer months. There's also an excellent dining room with views of the vineyards where the wines are paired with Canadian specialty foods. Turn off Highway 55 onto York Road and you'll come to **Château des Charmes** near St David's, which also gives tours. **Konzelmann Estate Winery** on Lakeshore Road (take Mary Street from Niagara-on-the-Lake) makes good wines as well.

Also on the outskirts of Niagara-on-the-Lake is the **Jackson-Triggs Niagara Estate Winery** (phone for opening times: 905/468 4637) designed by Toronto's KPMB architects. The winery is a departure from the mock-château style often found in the region. Another modern masterpiece is the Le Clos Jordanne Winery, designed by the 'star-chitect' Frank Gehry.

Other towns to target in the area are **Jordan** and **Vineland**, both good places to stop for a while. Jordan is home to Cave Spring Cellars and also the distinguished Inn on the Twenty Restaurant and Wine Bar, which serves locally produced wines matched with fine cuisine using top quality local ingredients. At Vineland Estates, the dining room has a distinct California air, located as it is overlooking the vineyard from an outdoor deck. Again, the cuisine pairs local wines and local ingredients and features a selection of Canadian farm cheeses.

Stratford

This delightful town of 28,000, 143km (93 miles) northwest of Toronto (a 90-minute drive), lives up to its name in every way. Not only does it host the well-known **Stratford Festival** from April to November, but it also has a style and

Shakespeare and Co

In 1830, a Canadian innkeeper named William Sargint decided to name his hostelry, which was located in the area of Huronia, the Shakespeare Inn, and he hung out a sign with a picture of the bard. The small village officially became Stratford in 1835, and the local river, of course, was called the Avon. In the early 1900s, a Stratford citizen, R. Thomas Orr, pushed the town council into rebuilding a crumbling dam, cleaning out some marshland, and creating a 72-hectare (175-acre) park. The new lake resulting from the dam was christened Lake Victoria.

Fifty years later, a journalist named Tom Patterson conceived the idea of an Ontario **Stratford Festival**, similar to the English original, and enlisted the help of Sir Tyrone Guthrie to achieve the dream. On 13 July 1953 the opening performance of *Richard III*, starring Sir Alec Guinness, was given in a huge tent and was a great success. Since then, the festival has drawn such international stars as Peter Ustinov, Dame Maggie Smith, Julie Harris, Irene Worth, and Christopher Plummer. The tent has long been replaced by three theaters.

bucolic atmosphere worthy of the bard's English birthplace – and though the play may be the thing, it is certainly not the only thing to enjoy here. William Shakespeare would probably have approved of the **Festival Theatre** at 55 Queen Street. It is shaped like a coronet, with a commodious, nearly circular seating area and convertible thrust stage.

A black swan, Stratford

Curtain times are announced by a trumpet fanfare played by musicians in Renaissance breeches, and between acts the audience can relax with a drink on the terrace. But this showpiece isn't the only theater in town. The **Avon Theatre** offers a traditional proscenium stage, while the smaller **Tom Patterson Theatre** features mainly experimental theater and jazz throughout the summer.

Around Stratford

Queen's Park, adjacent to the Festival Theatre, is pleasant for walking and picnicking before or after a play; swans and ducks grace its **Victoria Lake**. Across the footbridge in nearby Confederation Park, the **Gallery Stratford** (54 Romeo Street, tel: 519/271-5271; open Tue–Sun 10am–5pm) offers changing exhibitions focusing on Shakespearean themes, or simply on contemporary art.

If you follow the lake to the dam, you'll find a gate leading to the **Shakespearean Garden**, planted with botanicals that Shakespeare mentioned in his sonnets and plays. Note the bust of Shakespeare and the sundial, both presented by a former mayor of Stratford-upon-Avon in England.

Good food is the other reason to visit to Stratford. The Stratford Chefs School is here and there is a farmer's market early on Saturday morning. The two outstanding restaurants are **Rundles** (tel: 519/271-6442) and The **Old Prune** (tel: 519/271-5052). The first is more contemporary in look and ambience, the second, in a Victorian residence, is warm and comfortable. Both serve superb meals. The **Church Restaurant and the Belfry** (70 Brunswick Street, tel: 519/273-3424) has striking decor. It is located in a 19th-century church; diners sit in the oak-and-stone nave under the massive organ pipes, surrounded by Gothic-style stained-glass windows. The choir loft is now a cozy bar.

Just outside Stratford, the small town of **Shakespeare** has become an antiques center. Ten minutes south of Stratford, **St Mary's** is an interesting town where the massive 19th-century buildings are built of gray stone.

The Mennonite farm where traditional methods are still used

Mennonite Country

The pleasant countryside and villages northeast of Stratford are home to communities of German Mennonites that first became established in the area around turn of the 19th century. Head east on Highway 7 to **Kitchener-Waterloo**. Here you can stop at the downtown Farmer's Market, which begins at dawn Saturday morning and continues

The Elora Mill Inn

until early afternoon, for a glimpse – and a taste – of Mennonite life. You'll find savory cheeses, sausages, golden apple pies, and home-produced honey, along with colorful seasonal flowers. With its German heritage still very much alive, Kitchener is also famous for its lively Oktoberfest.

Up Highway 85, **Elmira** and **St Jacobs** are both small communities surrounded by Mennonite farms, and their country stores are well stocked with local crafts. Elmira was one of the first settlements, providing fertile farmland for the Mennonites in the early 1800s. Its quaint stores include Brox's Olde Town Village complex. Harness races are staged at Elmira Raceway, and each year the town celebrates spring with the Maple Syrup Festival, just as the sap is rising in the maple trees. Tiny St Jacobs, which was originally called Jacobstettel, has a touch of old-world charm. You'll find an interesting account of the Mennonite way of life on display in the **Meeting Place Museum**.

To the northeast, **Elora** holds a major arts festival in summer. Arts-and-crafts stores occupy the picturesque 19th-century limestone buildings that line Main Street, where the award-winning Elora Inn perches on the dramatic cliffs overlooking the Grand River rapids and falls. The gorge is a highlight and playground for white-water kayakers and fly fishermen. Hiking trails line the banks of the gorge and offer scenic views.

Nearby **Fergus** is a handsome town filled with 19th-century Scottish-style limestone buildings, and famous for its authentic Scottish Highland games held in August, with pipe bands, dancing, caber tossing, and tug-of-war contests.

Georgian Bay Area

The Huronia district around Georgian Bay, about 150km (90 miles) from Toronto, is a worthwhile area for a day or two's excursions. Near Midland, at **Ste-Marie Among the Hurons**, stockades, wood smoke, and costumed pioneer 'missionaries' provide a graphic portrait of the French mission to the Huron, established here in 1639 and lasting a

Georgian Bay coastline

decade. Rival Iroquois, envious of the lucrative Huron-French fur trade, attacked the mission, killing Father Daniel and 2,000 Huron in 1648. In 1649, 10km (6 miles) from the settlement, two Jesuit fathers, Brébeuf and Lalemant, were tortured to death along with many Hurons. The few remaining Jesuits abandoned their settlement and returned to Québec; contact with the First Nations was lost for 100 years.

Today, the stockaded village has been reconstructed and ebullient costumed students playing the roles of carpenter, gardener, priest, blacksmith, and members of the First Nations give a guided tour. See the dirt-floor Church of St Joseph (the burial site of the martyred missionaries Brébeuf and Lalemant), the blacksmith's forge, the apothecary's counter, a tepee, and a Huron-style sapling bark longhouse.

Don't miss the **museum** (open May–Oct 10am–5pm; admission fee) just outside the mission walls – a series of rooms constructed around a leafy artificial waterfall and woodland indoor courtyard. The exhibits display French and Indian artifacts from 17th-century France and Canada.

A mile or so east, on Highway 21 (on the eastern edge of Midland), you'll see the twin spires of the **Martyrs' Shrine**, a 20th-century monument to eight martyred missionaries, including the Jesuit priests from Sainte-Marie. A pathway uphill leads past bronze reproductions of the Stations of the Cross. Once inside the shrine, see paintings of suffering martyrs or – more pleasantly – look out at the vistas of the surrounding countryside.

Across from the shrine at **Wye Marsh Wildlife Centre** (open daily 9am–5pm; admission fee), naturalists lead tours along the boardwalks, pointing out the flourishing bird, animal, and plant life of the marsh. Better views can be had from an observation tower and also from an underwater window. There's also an indoor theater and display hall.

Cottage country

The Georgian Bay, Muskoka, and Haliburton regions are no longer untamed forest wildernesses. Thousands of cottages, ranging from rustic to luxurious, dot the area. Everyone in Ontario seems to have a country estate, even if it's only a humble cabin.

In the town of **Midland**, the **Huronia Museum** and another faithful copy of a Huron village illustrate the lifestyle of the Indians before the coming of the Jesuits. The village has palisades and a firing platform, and the aroma of drying fish. Carry a papoose on a wooden cradle-board, grind your own corn with round stones, or visit the medicine man's lodge if you aren't feeling well. Midland is the center for cruising the Georgian Islands – 30,000 of them. If you have time, take a **chartered boat trip** that follows the route of Champlain, Brulé, and La Salle.

At **Penetanguishene** (north on Highway 27) you can see the **British Naval and Military Establishments**, reconstructed to resemble those built by the British in 1817 to protect the Upper Great Lakes. Costumed guides enthusiastically demonstrate garrison life, performing their military duties with zeal. Schooner trips are offered, too.

The Georgian Triangle

About 150km (93 miles) north of Toronto is the **Georgian Triangle**, a destination for outdoor enthusiasts that is full of superlatives, including Ontario's largest ski area and the world's longest freshwater beach.

Hiking, mountain biking, and rock-climbing are popular summer activities. Winter sports enthusiasts can head for **Collingwood**, where Intrawest, the company responsible for developing Whistler Blackcomb in British Columbia, has developed **Blue Mountain**, an all-season resort complete with golf courses, ski-hill expansions, and a village full of shopping and restaurants. It helps that Georgian Bay is nearby, as is the **Bruce Trail**, a 770-km (480-mile) trail that traverses the scenic **Niagara Escarpment**. Although the enormity of the trail is daunting, hikers can opt to hike sections of the trail from many points in the area with the help of maps that can be picked up at visitor and tourist information centers.

Muskoka

When Torontonians want to take a break, they head for their cottages in the **Muskoka Lakes** – and it's worth taking a couple of days to do the same. There are thousands of lakes, acres of forest, and numerous resorts still catering to visitors. The cottages were built in the 19th century; people would arrive with their steamer trunks and stay for the season. **Gravenhurst** and **Bracebridge** are the two gateways to the region. **Port Carling** is the hub of the lakes; here the **Muskoka**

Snowboarding at Blue Mountain Resort, Collingwood

Lakes Museum gives insight into the region's history and development. Located in the center of Port Carling village the museum also organises annual events and walking tours of the area. **The Muskoka Boat and Heritage Centre**, which opened in 2006, features interactive exhibits about the history of watercraft with a boathouse where vessels are on display.

Huntsville has two major resorts, namely Deerhurst and Grandview Inn. Try, though, to make time to visit **Algonquin Park**, northeast of Huntsville, 4,800 sq km (3,000 sq miles) of wilderness for camping, fishing, and canoeing along the 1,600km (1,000 miles) of canoe routes. Here you might spy moose, beaver, and deer, and hear the cry of the loon. The most entrancing place to stay is Arowhon Pines (open May– Oct), which offers lakeside seclusion in comfortable cottages and cabins, and a wide range of sports.

Kingston

The main gateway to the Thousand Islands is **Kingston**, 240km (150 miles) northeast of Toronto, and it merits a visit for its magnificent setting on Lake Ontario (at the point where the St Lawrence River branches out northeastward) and for its historic town center built of gray stone. It's also a college town, for Queen's University, St Lawrence College, and the Royal Military College are all based here, swelling the year-round population of 60,000 to nearly 90,000.

Initially a First Nation, then a French-First Nation, trading post, the town of Kingston became a shipbuilding naval base during the War of 1812. Fort Henry was built in 1832 as the main military stronghold of Upper Canada, and from 1841 to 1844 Kingston became the capital of the United Province of Canada.

You can take the streetcar around town or enjoy walking or cycling. In summer, bicycles are available on or near the esplanade in front of domed City Hall on the waterfront. Folk-art and craft fairs and other events are held on this green esplanade in summer. Constructed of local limestone, Kingston's city hall boasts one of the finest examples of nineteenth century classical municipal architecture in Ontario. Behind City Hall, Market Square's outdoor **weekend market** is a splendid rendezvous for everyone, from families selling home-grown potatoes or raspberries to aging flower-children selling ceramics. The **Pumphouse Steam Museum** and the **Marine Museum** are both on Ontario Street near the waterfront.

The most touching historical site is perhaps **Bellevue House** (35 Centre Street; open Apr–May 10am–5pm, June–early-Sept 9am–6pm, early-Sept–Oct 10am–5pm; admission fee), a Victorian interpretation of a Tuscan villa beyond Macdonald Park. Prime Minister Sir John A. Macdonald lived here for a year, from 1848, with his dying wife and baby. Restored and furnished in its original style, the house exudes

A smile and sunflowers at the market, Kingston

both gentility and sadness, as the guides explain how the household was run based on Mrs Macdonald's needs.

Across the La Salle Causeway, **Fort Henry** (open May–Oct 10am–5pm; admission fee) stands out on a bluff. Here, student 'soldiers' perform 19th-century military drills. Guarded by Martello towers along the waterfront, Fort Henry was never attacked. The **Ceremonial Retreat** is an impressive military show, usually performed on Wednesday and Saturday evenings in July and August.

The Thousand Islands

Long a vacation playground for Americans and Canadians, the Thousand Islands are strung out from Kingston along the St Lawrence for nearly 80km (50 miles). If you try counting them, you'll probably come up with about 1,700 – from the merest rocky outcrop to islands big enough for a yacht

A house by the lake

club or two and a smattering of houses. Several boat lines from Kingston or nearby **Gananoque** offer day or half-day trips around the islands; the steamboat *Empress* even makes a luxury three-day cruise. The island scenery is striking, with dark green conifers and silvery birches set on grassy knolls amid gray and pinkish granite outcroppings. The build-

Friendly ferry captain

ings, all dubbed 'cottages' though ranging from simple shacks to rambling mansions, are all equally interesting. Guides point out **Millionaires' Row** and the places where Irving Berlin, John Foster Dulles, Helena Rubinstein, and others came to get away from it all.

Your boat will probably pass under the **International Bridge**, opened in 1938 by Franklin D. Roosevelt and William Lyon Mackenzie King. It required 10,000 liters (2,600 gallons) of light-green paint to achieve the artistic color you see today.

Boldt Castle (open May–Oct daily 10am–6.30pm; admission fee) is required viewing. The most famous of the millionaires' mansions, you'll find it either a marvel or a spooky Gothic monstrosity, according to your mood and taste. This turreted Rhenish folly might have been impressive, but it was never finished. George Boldt, the German magnate who owned the New York Waldorf-Astoria Hotel, built it at the turn of the 20th century as a gift for his wife. Louise Boldt died before the castle was finished, but today delighted visitors wander around the elaborate stone structure and vast, empty rooms imagining what might have been.

WHAT TO DO

SHOPPING

Toronto is a shoppers' paradise. The city has numerous famous brand-name stores, but it also has plenty of small boutiques. The vast network of underground passageways makes it a pleasure to shop, even in winter. Most stores accept credit cards, and be sure to ask about a refund (on the provincial tax) if you are taking the goods abroad.

Where to Shop

Torontonians do a lot of their shopping at the **Eaton Centre**, at Yonge and Dundas. Here, spread over four floors, you'll find more than 300 stores selling everything from men's and women's fashions to housewares, shoes, books, and leather goods. There are also plenty of restaurants and several food halls so that you can snack and rest as you go. Across Queen Street from the Eaton Centre, and linked by a covered footbridge, **HBC** is a good department store in which to look for Canadian designers and other traditional goods.

At the foot of York Street, **Queen's Quay Terminal** was once an old warehouse that has been transformed into a two-story shopping mall with more than 30 stores, plus a dance theater. This is more geared to tourists, but it does have a number of fine stores and galleries such as the sculpture-filled Museum of Inuit Art.

At 276 King Street West, the **Toronto Antique Centre** houses about 100 dealers selling fine silver, china and pottery, jewelry, furniture, prints, military memorabilia, antique sports equipment, and much more.

Queen Street West is the cutting-edge shopping street. Here you'll find small stores opened by young Canadian designers, plus an assortment of stores that range from antiquarian book dealers to funky secondhand furniture and clothes stores. West on Dundas, **Chinatown** is a good place to pick up small, inexpensive items, such as paper lanterns, embroidered slippers and woven baskets. **Kensington Market** specializes more in food, but check out the racks of vintage clothes on Augusta and Kensington Avenue.

Though famous, apart from the Eaton Centre, **Yonge Street** has little to offer except fast food outlets and a handful of nondescript stores, including several electronic discount stores. Bucking the trend is Urban Outfitters, at 235, a popular shop offering hip clothing for 20- and 30-somethings.

Bloor Street between Avenue Road and Yonge Street is the ultimate luxury shopping area, comparable to New York's Madison Avenue or Paris's rue du Faubourg Saint-Honoré. Head here if you can't live without a new Cartier watch, Yves St Laurent jacket, or Gucci bag.

Yorkville, north of Bloor along Cumberland Street and Yorkville Avenue, is another chic shopping area. You'll find classic designer fashions along with some younger, more modern looks from Canadian designers. The pretty Victorian buildings house all kinds of stores: art galleries, antiques and china shops, scent and

Fashion in Yorkville

soap shops, zany gift and greeting-card shops. Don't miss the small, elegant malls here: Hazelton Lanes and Cumberland Court.

It's also fun to explore the stores in different ethnic enclaves – along College Street in **Little Italy,** for instance, or along the Danforth in **Greektown**.

At the Sandra Ainsley Gallery

Arts and Crafts

Contemporary Canadian arts and crafts make excellent purchases for your collection or as mementos of your trip. In Toronto look for crafts at such stores as The Guild Shop on Cumberland Street, or the Arctic Bear on Yorkville Avenue. For a glimpse at national creativity visit Proud Canadian Design on Queen's Quay West. Prime Gallery on McCaul also has fine quality work. Du Verre on Queen Street West, specializes in beautiful glass objects.

The **Distillery Historic District** is a cobblestone village of recently restored Victorian industrial buildings and is entirely dedicated to arts, culture, and entertainment. Bookhou Design carries decorative objects and textile handbags, while Corktown Design offers one-of-a-kind handmade jewellery. Fawn Ceramics features handmade tiles and limited edition pottery. The Sandra Ainsley Gallery there has some spectacular glasswork, including pieces by the amazing Dale Chihuly. You can also find over 130 galleries and workshops in the historic warehouse at 401 Richmond.

The Art Gallery of Ontario has a good selection of crafts in their store, as do other museum shops. Many of these craft stores have contemporary jewelry as well. Also look for

Something for the bookworms

jewelry at such stores as Peter Cullman and Silverbridge on Cumberland Street or at 18 Karat in Village by the Grange on McCaul Street. For classic jewelry go to Birks and, of course, Tiffany & Co.

If you enjoy browsing for antiques, then go to the cluster of stores located around the Four Seasons Hotel in Yorkville; another pocket can be found on Queen Street West at Roncesvalles. For design and clothing stores with assorted stuff, explore the rest of Queen Street West. Also, don't miss the Toronto Antique Centre, which has 100 dealers with some very fine-quality artifacts at good prices, compared to what is usually charged in the US.

Canadians make great cold-weather gear and activewear. Check out what's offered at the Canadian chain Roots, on Yonge Street at the Eaton Centre, and Tilley Endurables in Queen's Quay Terminal and, for serious outdoor enthusiasts, Mountain Equipment Co-op on King Street West. Canadian furs and leather goods come in all qualities and price ranges. Traditionally, fur sales are held twice a year – in summer and in January – when you can negotiate a good deal. Start at A la Mode Regency Furs on Bathurst.

Toronto has many young fashion designers that are fun to check out. Look for such stores as Peach Berserk, Comrags, Lilith and Psyche, all on Queen Street West, and Lydia K and

Mercy at Model Citizen on Dundas Street. For coveted secondhand clothing including vintage Levi's and leather and
suede coats, explore Kensington Market.

Gift shopping

Gift shops sell all the amusing oddities you might want to
take back with you. Look for Oh Yes Toronto! on Yorkville
Avenue and in the Eaton Centre, plus Legends of the Game
on King Street West. The many boutiques in the Distillery
District also provide inspiration for gift shopping. The museum stores at the Art Gallery, ROM, and the McMichael
Collection are great sources for gifts too. There are also craft
shops and weekend markets from May to October in Mennonite country, particularly in Elora, Elmira, and St Jacobs.

You'll find some stores in Toronto that reflect Canada's
continuing cultural connections with the UK, such as Ash-
ley China on Bloor Street, which stocks a full range of china
and crystal, and seems to have terrific selections of, and

Contemporary Art

If you like passing time looking at (or buying) contemporary art or
sculpture, then spend an afternoon in the galleries in Yorkville along
Hazelton Avenue. Don't miss Gallery Gevik, Mira Godard, Miriam Shiell
and Nancy Poole's Studio. Queen Street West has now surpassed
Yorkville in galleries per capita, offering a number of small galleries
catering to the more alternative (and often more affordable) art scene.
An authentic soapstone carving or painting by a Native Canadian will
cost you plenty, but you can always look in galleries for a smaller, affordable sculpture or to simply enjoy the works on display. The major
gallery for Inuit art is Fehely Fine Arts on Hazelton. For a full listing of
what's happening in the art world, pick up a copy of *Slate*, the free
gallery guide.

prices for, English china in particular. For high-end shopping don't miss Holt Renfrew, which has a series of designer boutiques within the store; it is Toronto's Bloomingdale's. Canada has no embargo against Cuba, so you can purchase Cuban cigars in Toronto at such wonderful tobacconists as Winston & Holmes, but they cannot be taken to the US.

ENTERTAINMENT

There's plenty of evening entertainment in Toronto, although it's not exactly the city that never sleeps. Remember, the subway stops running at about 1.30am.

Music

Toronto is a terrific classical music town with a great number of small specialty groups. Besides the Toronto Symphony at the renovated Roy Thomson Hall, you'll want to see Tafelmusik Baroque Orchestra, which uses authentic period instruments, the Canadian Brass, or the Toronto Mendelssohn Choir, which gained its greatest fame for the soundtrack of Steven Spielberg's movie *Schindler's List*. The choir performs *The Messiah* each Christmas.

The Canadian Opera Company has a special reputation for outstanding performances of the Handel repertoire. The company's permanent home is the state-of-the-art Four Seasons Centre for the Performing Arts *(see page 42)*, which it shares with the National Ballet of Canada.

Other venues you can check out for musical events include Trinity-St Paul's on Bloor Street; Massey Hall, Victoria Street; the Glenn Gould Studio, Front Street; Toronto Centre for the Arts, North York; the University of Toronto's Walter Hall; and the Royal Conservatory of Music, Bloor Street.

Jazz flourishes in Toronto too. In late June jazz plays at 50-plus venues during the TD Canada Trust Jazz Festival. At other times check out the Montreal Bistro on Sherbourne. The Rivoli and The Rex on Queen Street West are other good bets for jazz or other eclectic performance art.

Toronto also has its fair share of first-rate dance companies, plus a theater specifically designed for dance, located at Queen's Quay. Besides the wonderful, classic National Ballet of Canada, at the Four Seasons Centre for the Performing Arts, modern companies to look out for include the Toronto Dance Theatre, Danny Grossman, and DanceMakers.

Jazz is a passion in Toronto

Theater

Toronto has become known for its theater, and it ranks third behind London and New York in the English-speaking world. The city doesn't have a Broadway, but it does have several historic theaters, as well as two or three ultra-modern performance centers, and, most importantly, a large number of thriving small theaters.

You'll find Broadway musicals or similar productions at The Royal Alexandra and the Princess of Wales theaters, both on King Street West; the Elgin and Winter Garden theaters on Yonge; Pantages on Victoria Street; and the Toronto Centre for the Arts on Yonge in North York. Canadian Stage, also known as CanStage, is the country's largest not-

The Princess of Wales Theater

for-profit theater company, which presents productions at the St Lawrence Centre and a smaller theatre at 26 Berkeley Street. Look out for performances by the smaller companies such as Buddies in Bad Times for alternative, gay-oriented drama; and the Factory Theatre, the Tarragon Theatre, and Theatre Passe Muraille for new works by Canadian playwrights. Lorraine Kimsa Theatre for Young People stages kids' entertainment.

Outside Toronto, **Stratford** *(see page 70)* is as well known on the North American continent as its English counterpart, not only for Shakespeare and productions of many other playwrights, but for jazz and musical comedy, too. At **Niagara-on-the-Lake** *(see page 67)*, George Bernard Shaw's plays take center stage during the Shaw Festival (April to November). It is the only theater festival in the world that specializes in Shaw, although the works of other playwrights are also performed.

Film

Film is another passion in Toronto, and the Toronto International Film Festival in September has become the second-largest in the world and many Canadian movies have won awards. If you want to see art and independent movies, check out the Cumberland and Cinematheque Ontario.

Comedy

Comedy is to Canada as apple pie is to America. Much of what Americans watch on TV was written or created by Canadians, including *Saturday Night Live* and *Kids in the Hall*. The breeding ground for so many North American comedians is also right here in Toronto, at Second City, which launched the careers of Dan Aykroyd and Mike Myers, and later (via SCTV) John Candy, Eugene Levy, Martin Short, and Rick Moranis. Look for comedy at Second City, The Laugh Resort on King Street West, and Yuk Yuk's on Yonge Street, which spawned Jim Carrey.

Bar Life

There are plenty of bars in Toronto. Among the popular sedate hotel bars, La Serre at the Four Seasons makes the best martinis in town; the rooftop bar at the Hyatt has been a favorite haven for the city's literary lights for years; and the Chartroom at the Harbour Castle has great views of the lake.

For cocktails with a view, head to Horizons on the top of the CN Tower, or to Panorama on top of the Manulife Centre on Bloor Street West.

Downtown, many restaurants have up-front bars where an after-work crowd gathers – Acqua and Jump, for example. John Street is lined with bars with outdoor terraces that are crowded in summer. Check out Al Frisco's and Montana's to start, and then head round

Nightclubs

Dance clubs for the young and fashionable are jam-packed on weekends. You can find them in the nightlife district that has grown up around Adelaide, Richmond and King streets near John Street. Current hot spots include Fluid Lounge, Fusion and Red Drink Boutique on Richmond, Power and Limelight on Adelaide, and Industry and the über-chic Mint et Menthe on King.

the corner to the cavernous Alice Fazooli's on Adelaide. On Queen West is The Paddock, an art deco bistro and bar with lots of atmosphere and an extensive wine list and a gathering place for playwrights and actors. If you're a wine lover, look for Vintages on King Street. Fans of Wayne Gretzky will want to stop at his establishment on Blue Jays Way. The Drake Hotel, on Queen Street West, is a chic meeting place for the art and literary crowd.

Toronto also has a number of English-style pubs, such as the Duke of Westminster at First Canadian Place. Don't overlook the Dora Keogh on the Danforth for some true Irish spirit. In Little Italy, the fashionable spot is Bar Italia on College Street, but there are plenty of others (Corso Italia and Souz Dal). Uptown Centro and North 44° both have appealing, comfortable bars.

SPORTS

Until the opening of the Air Canada Centre, they used to say that there was only one shrine in Toronto and that was Maple Leaf Gardens, home of the Toronto hockey team. Indeed, it sometimes seems that Canadians learn to skate before they learn to walk, and ice hockey is certainly the most popular national sport.

Canadians are generally active, and there are plenty of opportunities for visitors to engage in a variety of activities in Toronto, from jogging and cycling on the waterfront trails to canoeing and skating. Top-notch hotels often provide full fitness facilities, including swimming pools, and many stores rent cycles and other equipment.

Participant Sports

Toronto has been rated the number one **bicycling** city in North America; cycling is a common way of getting around

Rollerbladers take a break on Centre Island

town. The best place to cycle, though, is through the Toronto Islands. Visitors can rent bikes from Wheel Excitement (tel: 416/260-9000) and Toronto Island Bicycle Rental (tel: 416/203-0009).

Thirty municipal parks have **tennis** facilities (tel: 416/392-1111), the most convenient locations are High Park and Rosedale Park. Tennis Canada (tel: 416/665-9777; <www.tenniscanada.com>) aims to develop the sport nationally.

Many Torontonians have a Scottish heritage, so there are plenty of good **public golf courses**. The RBC Canadian Open championship is played at a different venue each year, including Glen Abbey, about 30 minutes west of Toronto in Oakville, Angus Glenn in Markham north of Toronto, and the Hamilton Golf and Country Club. There are plenty of good public courses where green fees are less expensive, notably Don Valley, Humber Valley, and Tam O'Shanter. Private clubs are usually accessible, especially during the week (if you can prove membership to a golf club at home, you can usually obtain special privileges).

Toronto can get steamy in summer, but there are plenty of **swimming pools** to cool off with a dip in the water. Most hotels have pools, and the city operates six or so pools in municipal parks as well (the most convenient being High Park and Rosedale). The YMCA offers a day-pass for all its sports facilities; the University also opens its pool to the public at certain times. Community recreation centers have pools too. For pool information, call 416/392-1111. There are sandy public beaches in the east end and on the Toronto Islands, which are sometimes closed due to pollution. Water quality readings are posted.

Toronto is also one of the few cities where you can go **sailing** or **canoeing** on your own. If you're qualified, you can rent a sail or powerboat at Queen's Quay Yachting at 275

Around the Islands are attractive sailing waters

Queen's Quay West (tel: 416/203-3000. Canoes and kayaks can be rented at Harbourfront Canoe and Kayak Centre, 283a Queen's Quay West (tel: 416/203-2277; <www.paddletoronto.com>). For additional yachting and sailing information, contact the Canadian Yachting Association (tel: 613/545-3044).

Maple Leafs supporters
on a winning day

In winter, you can **cross-country ski** in municipal parks. For information about rentals, contact Toronto Parks (tel: 416/392-1111).

Ice-skating is a popular pastime; in winter the reflecting pool in Nathan Phillips Square, in front of City Hall, is converted into an ice rink. Other rinks are at Harbourfront and in the parks. The most romantic is at Grenadier Pond in High Park, where vendors sell chestnuts from glowing braziers.

Spectator Sports

Hockey is *the* national spectator sport, and children learn it as a matter of course. The Toronto Maple Leafs (members of the National Hockey League) play home-based matches regularly from October to April at Air Canada Centre.

Curling, a kind of lawn bowls on ice, is a relaxing sport to watch, especially if you have a warm drink in hand. Canada is one of the few places where you can witness the sport; contact any ice rink and they'll tell you when the next game will be.

Baseball gets a big play in Toronto. Firm favorites in the city are the local Blue Jays of the American League East. In 1992, they became the first non-US team to win the World Series, making them the pride of Toronto. They won again

Big hitter

As a professional ball player, Babe Ruth hit his first home run in 1914 at a game at Hanlan's Point on the Toronto Islands.

the following year, but then the New York Yankees took over. See the Blue Jays at Rogers Centre. For tickets to Blue Jays events, telephone 416/341-1234.

Although invented in Canada in 1891, **Basketball** arrived in Toronto when the local team, the Raptors, played its first season in 1997. The team plays at Air Canada Centre.

Football is played by Canadian rules on a 100-m (110-yd) field – longer than the 100-yd US version – under the auspices of the Canadian Football League, whose great annual event, the Grey Cup, is hotly disputed in an east–west confrontation. The big-league home team is The Argonauts (CFL football). They play at Rogers Centre.

Lacrosse is the official national Canadian sport. Semi-pro games are regularly played in Toronto.

Horseracing takes place at Woodbine Racetrack in Etobicoke. The Queen's Plate is run in June or July, the Canadian International in the fall, and the North America Cup in mid-June. Harness racing is held in spring and fall. Other races are run at Fort Erie Racetrack, about 160km (100 miles) outside Toronto.

TORONTO FOR CHILDREN

Kids will find plenty of things to do in Toronto, and plenty of organizations and festivals cater specifically to them. What follows is a summary of the attractions that have the greatest kid appeal, not necessarily in any given order of preference.

Sure-fire hits include the **Ontario Science Centre** for its zillion fun interactive exhibits and many dynamic science demonstrations; the **Toronto Zoo** for the animal feeding and wonderful pavilions and paddocks where kids can watch animals in their natural habitats; and **Canada's Wonderland** for the water park, roller coasters, go-karts, and other entertainments. But watch out for the tempting video games, which can add greatly to the already high ticket price.

Ontario Place makes for an entertaining afternoon – those under 12 have a great time at the **Children's Playground**. **Harbourfront** caters to families and kids with a whole array of creative crafts, games, and special events. Kids also like the model boat pond, the ice rink, and going for a cruise, or if they're older, taking out a canoe. Taking the ferry to the islands with bicycles in tow can make a lovely day out. Smaller children will enjoy the old-fashioned amusement park and carousel at **Centreville**. At the **CN Tower**, kids are much more likely than adults are to dance on the glass floor at the top – there's also plenty to entertain them at the base.

Sure-fire fun at the Science Centre

Top landmarks: Rogers Centre and the CN Tower

Top hits at the **Royal Ontario Museum** are the dinosaur exhibits and the spooky Bat Cave. **Fort York** amuses kids with the drama of the drills and cacophonous musket and cannon firing. Athletic-minded youngsters will enjoy the **Hockey Hall of Fame,** where they can practice shooting and goal keeping, or don some pads and take up the challenge of stopping Mark Messier from scoring; the Honour Roll and the Stanley Cup may also impress them. Along the same lines, a tour of **Rogers Centre** *(see page 34)* is high on many chidrens' lists.

At **Black Creek Pioneer Village,** children can watch artisans make barrels and bake bread. **Casa Loma** can appeal to their imaginations with its secret passageways, handsome stables, and fantasy turrets. Older children will enjoy the **CHUMCity tour** and a visit to the **CBC Building**.

On Sunday afternoons there are special cushion concerts at Harbourfront geared towards children. Harbourfront also hosts a number of children's festivals, storytelling and programs. Go to <www.harbourfrontcentre.com> for listings. The **Lorraine Kimsa Theatre for Young People,** 165 Front Street East at Sherbourne (tel: 416/862-2222), presents acclaimed stage performances for and by children between October and May.

Calendar of Events

The following list covers just some of the dozens of special annual events. Please check times and places with the local tourist office *(see page 121)* or newspapers or listings magazines *(see page 117)*.

January Toronto International Boat Show.

February Toronto Winterfest celebrates the cold season with ice-skating, ice sculpting, snow play, and a lot more.

May Green Toronto Festival transforms Yonge and Dundas Square, offering up children's activities, locally grown food and over 100 exhibits. The CONTACT Toronto Photography Festival, at various venues across the city <www.contactphoto.com>.

June TD Canada Trust Toronto Jazz Festival swings for 10 days at 50 different venues around town. Toronto International Dragon Boat Race Festival includes races in giant Asian-style boats, plus cultural entertainment. Lesbian and Gay Pride Week celebrates the gay community with theater, film, and other entertainment culminating in a parade.

July Canada Day – the nation's birthday. Parties and fireworks. Caribana is 10 days of Caribbean dance, music, food, and parades. Fringe of Toronto Festival brings out theater lovers for 10 days to see a variety of performances around town. Molson Indy Car Race at Exhibition Place. Beaches International Jazz Festival.

August The Canadian National Exhibition. One big party that goes on for 18 days, with midway rides, agricultural exhibits, entertainment, and the Canadian Air Show.

September The Toronto International Film Festival. Directors and stars turn out for the screening of over 400 films. The RBC Canadian Open Golf championship – visit <www.thecanadianopen.ca> for tournament location.

October The International Festival of Authors takes over Harbourfront for 10 days.

November The Royal Agricultural Winter Fair and Royal Horse Show takes over Exhibition Place for 12 days.

December Cavalcade of Lights is an annual event that illuminates the city. Kensington Market Festival of Lights marks the winter solstice.

EATING OUT

The ethnic communities that have grown up since the 1970s have charged the food scene in Toronto with excitement, converting it from a meat-and-potatoes town into a city with a colorful, flavorful, cosmopolitan banquet table. There's scarcely a national cuisine that you can't savor.

Notes on Dining

Unless you want to pay a high price for breakfast, don't dine at your hotel. Instead, walk around the corner to either a deli or a coffee shop, or to one of the many coffee houses where you can secure a tasty muffin, croissant, or bagel. Brunch is a combination lunch/breakfast that is often served on weekends only. This can be a gargantuan affair at the top hotels like the Four Seasons and the Intercontinental, but it's worth it. At lunchtime, do as the Torontonians do, and grab a cup of soup, a pizza slice or a massive sandwich or salad at any of the takeout emporiums. In summer, eat it outside in one of the squares or pocket parks; in winter, many takeouts have a few tables, or if they're located in an underground mall they'll have large sitting areas. If you enjoy sitting down for a formal lunch, there are plenty of options – and the tab will be smaller than it would be at dinner.

> ### Tax and Tips
>
> Taxes can add a lot to the check – 8 percent provincial tax, 7 percent gst, and 17 percent on alcohol. Tipping 15 percent on top of the pre-tax check is customary.

Afternoon tea can be enjoyed at such upmarket places as the Four Seasons and the King Edward Hotel, or at the tucked-away Red Tea Box on 676 Queen Street West, with a wide range of organic teas, and at La Tea Da, a traditional tea room at 2305 Queen Street East in The Beaches neighborhood.

Dinner can range in price from very little to a lot, depending on where you choose to eat *(see pages 132–142)*. Torontonians are not generally late-night diners, so some restaurants stop serving at 10pm. If you're looking for after-hours dining, your best bet is Chinatown or the Danforth, where many of the restaurants stay open until 2am or later. Certain neighborhoods have a distinct ethnic tilt – Chinatown along Dundas and Spadina, Little Italy along College Street between Euclid and Shaw. There's also a cluster of Ukrainian restaurants on Bloor west of Keele and Little India along Gerrard East. In general, restaurants in Yorkville are expensive and not worth the price. There are some good, value-for-money restaurants on Baldwin Street between Beverley and McCaul streets, ranging from French and Italian to Indonesian. Queen Street West also has a stretch of inexpensive Bohemian-style eateries.

Out to lunch

Visit a Niagara vineyard

Dinner reservations are recommended, and at the top restaurants they should be made well in advance for a weekend night or a public holiday. Note that Torontonians tend to be a little more formal than Americans are, so you might be more comfortable if you dress casual-but-chic for dinner. Most places do not insist on a jacket and tie for gentlemen. Note also that all restaurants are non-smoking.

The Cuisine

It's hard to articulate a distinct Canadian cuisine. Certainly there are some local ingredients that help identify it. The coastal regions of Nova Scotia and British Columbia have terrific seafood – Pacific and Atlantic salmon, Prince Edward Island mussels, New Brunswick lobsters, and Malpeque oysters – while Manitoba and inland Canada have some delicious freshwater fish as well. Great local meats and cheeses are available in Ontario from a variety of farms – Woolwich Farm goat cheese, Québec foie gras, Alberta beef, and Ontario lamb – and there's also plenty of game, such as Yukon caribou and Ontario pheasant.

The best places to sample such Canadian ingredients are Canoe, Tundra, and the premier restaurant at the Fairmont Royal York Hotel, where indigenous meals are paired with a wine list of more than 125 Canadian wines from 28 wineries.

In recent years the food scene has been transformed by such great chefs as Susur Lee at Susur and his more approachable off-shoot, Lee; Jamie Kennedy at JK Wine Bar and the Gardiner Museum of Ceramic Art; Chris McDonald at Avalon; Mark McEwan at North 44° and Bymark; Marc Thuet at Bistro and Bakery Thuet; Pat Riley at Perigée; and Manuel Vilela at Chiado. These chefs have brought dining in Toronto to a new height. Make plans to go to at least one of them if you can.

The revolutionizing of the average Torontonian palate, however, was accomplished by the many immigrants who arrived and opened restaurants to serve their fellow countryfolk – the Chinese, the Italians, the Portuguese, the Greeks, the Caribbean Islanders, the Thais, and many more. Thanks to them, much of the 'new Canadian' cuisine has been borrowed from each and every one of these traditions.

Niagara Vintages

Canadian wineries, particularly those around Niagara, are thriving. They attract people to their vineyards and associated restaurants, where they pair their wines with local Canadian specialties such as Prince Edward Island mussels, Ontario lamb, and Bay of Fundy salmon. There are three designated Ontario viticultural areas – the Niagara Peninsula, Pelee Island, and Lake Erie's North Shore. The Niagara wine region is closest to Toronto. It produces good, traditional varieties – chardonnays, Rieslings, Gewurtztraminers, cabernets, merlots, and pinot noirs.

But it is this region's ice wine that has achieved world recognition. Canada is the No. 1 producer of this elixir, which enhances every dessert (except those made with chocolate). Ice wine is so expensive because it is made with frozen grapes; it takes about five times as many grapes to make one bottle as a standard varietal. A bottle of this nectar makes a perfect souvenir.

Drinks

Torontonians appreciate beer. There are popular Canadian beers made by Molson and Labatt, but a number of local brewpubs, such as Amsterdam on King Street and Steam Whistle Brewing at the Roundhouse near Rogers Centre offer far superior microbrewed beer. Although wine is distributed by the Liquor Control Board, which limits the selection, many restaurants have superb lists, made up of wines from all over the world as well as local Ontario varieties. The Niagara region has become internationally renowned for its ice wine; while you're here you really should try some with a dessert *(see page 103)*.

The legal drinking age in Ontario is 19. You may be asked for photo identification proving your date of birth (a passport is usual for non-Canadian citizens). For the best bars in town, *see pages 91–2.*

Black Bull Tavern, one of the city's oldest pubs

HANDY TRAVEL TIPS

An A–Z Summary of Practical Information

A

ACCOMMODATIONS (See also YOUTH HOSTELS)

Tourism Toronto *(see page 122)* will provide an up-to-date listing of accommodations in Toronto. It is always advisable to make reservations in advance, regardless of the season, because Toronto attracts a great number of conventions.

Hotels. Toronto hotels are expensive *(see page 107)*, and additional charges for parking (around C$25) make them even more so.

Bed & Breakfasts. This is an option that may yield some savings – and it will surely allow for a different perspective on the city and its residents. B&Bs should be represented by an agency, which ensures good standards. For details contact: Toronto Bed & Breakfast, 253 College Street (PO Box 269), Toronto, ON, M5T 1R5; tel: (705) 738-9449, <www.torontobandb.com>. Downtown Toronto Association of Bed & Breakfast Guesthouses; tel: (416) 410-3938, <www.bnbinfo.com>. Bed & Breakfast Homes of Toronto, Box 46093, College Park Post Office, 777 Bay Street, Toronto, ON, M5G 2P6; tel: (416) 363-6362. Prices for a double room with bath start at C$90 and rise to C$200. Average price is C$120.

AIRPORTS

Toronto is served by **Lester B. Pearson International** (tel: 416/247-7678), 27km (18 miles) northwest of the city. It currently has two terminals: the new Terminal 1 and Terminal 3, Terminal 2 was demolished in 2008. An expansion of airport facilities is scheduled for completion by 2010. Note that on flights from Canada to the US (international airports), passengers go through US customs as they check in for their flight (and not after they have landed in the US).

Toronto Island Airport, off Harbourfront, is for small aircraft only.

The least expensive but most time-consuming way to get downtown is via express bus to the Islington, Yorkdale, and York Mills subway stations. The buses operate every 40 minutes, from about

7am to midnight, and cost C$2.75. Regular shuttle services also operate every 20 minutes between the airport and many downtown hotels; depending on traffic, this trip takes about 35 minutes and will cost around C$16. The most expensive choice is by taxi, which will cost about C$40–60 depending on your final destination.

B

BUDGETING FOR YOUR TRIP

Toronto is the most expensive city in Canada, but relatively cheap compared to other large US cities. However, prices listed below are subject to change – along with the strength of the Canadian dollar.

Accommodations. Hotel rates range from C$100 a night per room in a good value hotel to C$400 for the full service at say, the Four Seasons. B&Bs are a less expensive option, offering rooms for an average C$120. For other inexpensive options, see YOUTH HOSTELS.

Meals. If you want to save money, don't have breakfast at your hotel unless it's included in the price of the room. Instead, walk around the corner to a deli or a coffee shop. Lunch is always less expensive than dinner; depending on where you choose to eat, prices range from a couple of dollars for a slice of pizza to C$30 or more. Dinner can range from C$15 at a Chinese or similar ethnic restaurant, to C$30 at a typical bistro, to C$50 plus at higher-end eateries.

Transportation. Air fares are least expensive in spring, fall, and winter off-peak periods and most expensive during the summer and major holidays such as Christmas and Easter. The cheapest fare is usually an Advance Purchase or Apex <www.apextrav.com>, which generally requires a minimum stay of 7–14 nights and must be purchased at least 21 days in advance. If you want to save the most money, you're advised to try the bucket shops operated by consolidators who sell discounted fares even during peak season. Some airlines and major tour operators offer all-inclusive flight and accommodations 'city breaks,' which are often cheaper than purchasing airfare and accommodations separately. If you want to travel further in North America, then purchase an airpass before leaving home. Most airlines offer them. (See also AIRPORTS)

Transportation within Toronto costs C$2.75 per subway ride, although your best bet is to buy five tokens for the cost of less than four rides. Children 2–12 pay 70¢ or C$5 for 10. There's also a day pass for C$9 – it can be used from 9.30am on weekdays or from 6am on Saturday – which converts on Sunday into a family pass, allowing two adults and up to four children to travel all day. Always pick up a transfer, which allows you to switch from subway to bus-streetcar and vice-versa for free. For information tel: (416) 393-4636.

Entertainment and incidentals. A standard coach tour will cost around C$30, a harbor cruise around C$20. The top-rated museums charge C$10–12 admission; note, though, that some have free admission on certain days or at certain times. For theater performances at major venues, expect to pay anything from C$20 to C$100; for classical musical concerts C$15–70; opera C$35–$130. Most other incidentals will cost less here than in Europe or the US.

C

CAR RENTAL/HIRE

Consider renting a car only if you want to make excursions outside the city.

To rent a car, you must be over 23 years old (a surcharge may be levied if you are under 25) and possess a current driver's license. Visitors from non–English-speaking countries may need a translation of their license as well as the original document itself. Major rental-car companies are located at the airport and downtown; two well-known firms are Budget (tel: 1-800-268-8900) and National Tilden (tel: 1-800-387-4747). The average daily rate starts at C$45, weekly rates at C$200-plus including unlimited mileage. Rates do vary from company to company, so shop around. Note any drop-off charges if you don't return it to the original rental office. Some car rental companies don't allow you to leave the province in which the car was rented. And if you want to tour and drop the car off in another province – assuming that you find a company that allows this – you can be charged as much as C$1,000. You may be asked to choose between returning the car with a full tank of gasoline, or paying for a full tank in advance and returning the car with an empty tank.

Your own auto insurance, plus the insurance provided if you pay with certain credit cards, may be all the coverage you need for a rental car, but contact your insurance company before rejecting the car rental company's insurance. Usually collision is covered by your own auto insurance or by the credit card company. Liability, however, may not be, although a car booked from abroad will have some third-party liability insurance; if you consider this inadequate, car-rental agencies offer extended third-party liability protection for an extra charge.

CLIMATE AND CLOTHING

Though summer days tend to be hot and humid, you may hit a cool period – even in July – so you should always have a jacket or sweater for the evening. A light raincoat and hat and/or umbrella are needed as well. In winter, be prepared for the cold with heavy woolen or fur coats, warm sweaters, hats, gloves, and boots or galoshes. The wind blows off the lake with a ferocity that can hurt. Canadians in general dress a little more formally at better restaurants than their American neighbors do.

CRIME AND SAFETY

While Toronto is still known for its miraculously low crime rate compared to other big cities, you're still advised to take the usual precautions. Be on the lookout for pickpockets in crowded concourses and the subway, lock your car and hotel room, and deposit valuables in the hotel safe. Steer clear of parks at night and use good judgement in any area that looks seedy.

CUSTOMS AND ENTRY REQUIREMENTS

US citizens must now have a passport to show the Canadian officials when entering the country and the US authorities when returning. A driver's license is not accepted as identification. British subjects and citizens of Ireland, Australia, New Zealand, and South Africa also need passports to enter Canada. A return or onward ticket and enough money to cover your stay is also required. Citizens from most other countries require visas. Apply at your local Canadian embassy or consulate.

Customs limitations are as follows (if you are over 19): 200 cigarettes *or* 50 cigars *or* 2kg tobacco, 1.5 liters of wine, 1.14 liters of spirits, plus C$60 worth of gifts. Both arriving and departing passengers should report any money and checks exceeding C$10,000.

D

DRIVING

Canadians drive on the right, and there is little that will surprise anyone who drives in Western countries. In the city it is best to walk and use public transportation. Outside the city, the roads are good and fast. If you're headed for the Muskoka Lakes in summer or fall, avoid leaving on Friday or returning on Sunday afternoon when traffic is heavy.
Rules and regulations. The most important rules to observe are the wearing of seatbelts in front and back seats; speed restrictions (50 km/h or 30 mph in the city; 100/110 km/h or 60/70 mph on highways; 80 km/h or 50 mph on regular country roads; and 40 km/h or 25 mph in school and central urban districts); not driving while intoxicated, and parking regulations. Penalties (including towing) are stiff. You must stop at pedestrian crosswalks that are marked by overhead signs and a large painted X. If you are following a streetcar and it stops, stop well back from the rear doors so that passengers can exit easily and safely. Don't pass bright yellow school buses *in either direction* when passengers are getting *off or on*. Watch for the flash-

ing red signals on the bus. At most traffic lights you can turn right on a red signal after stopping, unless a sign states to the contrary.

Fuel costs. Gas (petrol) is cheaper in North America than elsewhere in the world. Expect to pay around C$1 a liter for regular 87-octane gas. Self-service stations are usually cheaper than full service stations.

Parking. It can be impossible to find on-street parking downtown – or in exclusive residential neighborhoods, where parking is reserved for residents. Never park alongside a fire hydrant. In Toronto, there is usually no parking or waiting on main streets during rush hours (7–9am and 4–6pm). Establish in advance what parking facilities your hotel can offer (most hotels and smart restaurants have valet parking). There are a number of large underground parking lots throughout the city: Ask the hotel concierge for details. Generally those marked with a green 'P' are the least expensive.

If you need help. It's worth joining your local affiliate of the Canadian Automobile Association, which has reciprocal agreements in many countries. CAA provides emergency towing service plus touring information, including maps. For information, contact the main CAA office at 1145 Hunt Club Road, Suite 200, ON, K1V 0Y3; tel: (800) 268-3750 (toll-free in the US and Canada), <www.caa.ca>. There is another CAA office at 60 Commerce Valley Drive East, Thornhill, ON, L3T 7P9; tel: (905) 771-3111.

Road signs. These are generally familiar, but foreign visitors may be unfamiliar with the two following:

Divided highway	Dual carriageway
Rotary	Circle/Roundabout

E

ELECTRICITY

Canada uses 110-volt 60-cycle AC. Plugs are generally small, flat, and two-pronged or three-pronged with flat and round pins. Visitors from overseas will need a plug adapter.

EMBASSIES, CONSULATES, AND HIGH COMMISSIONS

Australia: Consulate General, 175 Bloor Street East, Suite 1100, (at Church Street) Toronto, ON, M4W 3R8; tel: (416) 323-1155.

Republic of Ireland: Consulate General, 20 Toronto Street, Toronto, ON, M5C 2B8; tel: (416) 366-9300.

New Zealand: Consulate, 225 MacPherson Avenue, Toronto, ON, M4V 1A1; tel: (416) 947-9696.

South Africa: Consulate General, 110 Sheppard Avenue East, Toronto, ON, M2N 6Y8; tel: (416) 944-8825 ext 24.

UK: Consulate General, Suite 1910, College Park, 777 Bay Street, Suite 2800, Toronto, ON, M5G 2G2; tel: (416) 593-1290.

US: Consulate General, 360 University Avenue, Toronto, ON, M5G 1S4; tel: (416) 595-1700.

EMERGENCIES

Dial **911** for the police, ambulance, or fire department.
Dial **0** (zero) for the operator.

G

GAY AND LESBIAN TRAVELERS

Toronto is a sophisticated city and open to gay men and lesbians. The gay community's bars, restaurants, and other services are located along Church, south of Wellesley. For information pick up a copy of the weekly *Xtra* available free at many bookstores and at the Glad Day Bookshop, 598A Yonge Street, 2nd and 3rd floors; tel: (416) 961-4161 or (877) 783-3725 (toll free).

GETTING THERE

By Air

From the US. Air Canada has direct flights from most major cities in the United States. US Air, American, Delta, Northwest, and United all operate a limited number of direct flights to Toronto.

From the UK. British Airways, Air Canada, Air India, and Virgin Atlantic operate flights from London and from Manchester and Glasgow. Zoom, Thomas Cook and MyTravel operate charter flights.

From the Republic of Ireland. Aer Lingus flies from Shannon. Otherwise, transit via London.

From Australia and New Zealand. Air Canada has agreements with Qantas and Air New Zealand flying from Sydney and Auckland to Toronto with stops en route in Honolulu and also Fiji.

From South Africa. Several different airlines operate from Cape Town and Johannesburg using different access routes – Swissair via Zurich, South African Airways via Miami or New York; from Cape Town Air Canada flies via Frankfurt and Delta via New York. British Airways flies from Johannesburg via London.

By Rail

Amtrak links New York with Toronto via Albany, Buffalo, and Niagara Falls (11hr 30min). It also operates from Chicago via Port Huron (12hr 30min). Trains arrive at Union Station, which is connected to the subway. Like airline seats, rail seats may be discounted if you purchase them in advance. Always ask about special fares or discounts. Rail passes for unlimited travel within a set period are offered to foreign visitors. Call your local Amtrak representative at 800-USA-RAIL (800-872-7245 toll-free in the US and Canada, <www.amtrak.com>).

By Bus

Greyhound/Trailways (tel: 1-800-231-2222 toll-free in the US and Canada, <www.greyhound.com>) operates from almost anywhere in the US across the border into Canada. Buses arrive at the downtown Metro Coach Terminal on Bay Street at Dundas, within walking distance of the subway. The bus may be faster and cheaper than the train and its route more flexible if you want to stop along the way, but it's also more cramped, toilet facilities are meager, and meals are taken at somewhat depressing rest stops. Foreign travelers can purchase an Ameripass (it must be bought outside the US) for unlimited travel within a set period. Phone the Greyhound representative in your own country for more information.

By Car

Toronto is 154km (96 miles) from Buffalo, 795km (495 miles) from New York, 859km (534 miles) from Chicago, and 911km (566 miles) from Boston. The major crossing points into Canada are Detroit–Windsor; Port Huron–Sarnia; Buffalo–Fort Erie; Niagara Falls, NY–Niagara Falls, Ontario; and Niagara Falls, NY–Lewiston, Ontario.

GUIDES AND TOURS

Trolley and bus tours. Hop-on, hop-off bus tours are operated by Olde Town Toronto Tours (tel: 416/614-0999) aboard double-deckers, with tours to Niagara Falls. Gray Line (tel: 416/594-3310) operates standard-issue bus tours as well.

Walking and cycling tours. For informative walking and cycling tours of neighborhoods, one in Chinatown includes a *dim sum* lunch, call Taste of the World Tours (tel: 416/923-6813). Haunted Streets of Downtown runs 'ghost' tours of Toronto (tel: 416/487-9017).

Cruises and boat tours. Toronto Tours (tel: 416/869-1372) runs one-hour tours of the harbor and islands during summer. They leave from Queen's Quay West at the foot of York Street. A most beautiful experience can be had aboard *The Challenge*, a three-masted 29-m (96-ft) schooner, which sails several times during the day. For information, call the Great Lakes Schooner Company, 249 Queens Quay West; tel: (416) 260-6355.

Helicopter tours. National Helicopters operates from the Toronto Island Airport. Tel: (416) 361-1100 or 1-866-361-1100 for details.

HEALTH AND MEDICAL CARE (see also EMERGENCIES)

The quality of health care is high in Toronto, but you will have to pay for it – and it will be expensive. Therefore, make sure that you have purchased adequate health coverage in a standard travel package from an insurance company or a travel agent before you leave home.

Other than the annoying blackflies and mosquitoes (and they can be extremely pesky up in the woodlands and around lakes in June/July), there are no special health problems in Ontario. If you intend to sunbathe, take the usual sunscreen precautions – the sun can burn you on a lake as fiercely as it might in the Aegean Sea. Pharmacies, or drugstores, are generally open 9am–10 or 10.30pm, Monday to Saturday.

For **emergency medical care** call or visit The Toronto General Hospital; tel: (416) 340-3111 or (416) 340-3946. There are entrances at 200 Elizabeth Street and 150 Gerrard Street West.

HOLIDAYS

When a holiday falls on a Sunday, the following Monday is often observed as a holiday as well. There are 10 statutory holidays, when all government offices and most businesses are closed:

1 January	New Year's Day
Third Monday in February	Family Day (Ontario Only)
Variable	Good Friday
Variable	Easter Monday
Monday before 25 May	Victoria Day
1 July	Canada Day
First Monday in August	Simcoe Day
First Monday in September	Labour Day
Second Monday in October	Thanksgiving Day
25 December	Christmas Day
26 December	Boxing Day

L

LANGUAGE

Even though Canada and the province of Ontario are officially bilingual and every government pamphlet or document is printed in both

English and French, English is Toronto's language. Still, in various Toronto neighborhoods, you're likely to hear Italian, German, Chinese, Urdu, and so on. Americanisms have definitely crept into this once very Scottish and British part of the world, although in many cases British rather than American terms are still used.

LIQUOR LAWS

The main place to buy liquor (spirits) and wines is in LCBOs (stores run by the Liquor Control Board of Ontario), of which there are several in every city, usually open 10am to 6pm Monday through Saturday. Some LCBOs are open later and on Sundays; check the Yellow Pages for addresses. There are independent wine shops, which are only allowed to stock Canadian wines. The primary sales channel for beer in Ontario is The Beer Store, which carries a wide range of Canadian and foreign beers and has 21 retail outlets in Toronto. The minimum drinking age is 19, and drinking hours in licensed establishments are 11am–2am daily. It is against the law to carry around an open container of any type of alcohol. Note, there is no longer any smoking permitted inside pubs and bars.

LOST AND FOUND

The Toronto Transit Commission's Lost Articles is at the Bay Street subway station; tel: (416) 393-4100. It is open 8am–5pm Monday through Friday.

MAPS

Good maps of Ontario and some city maps are available from the Ministry of Tourism (see TOURIST INFORMATION). Among city maps, the laminated *Streetwise Toronto* is recommended, although there are plenty of other possibilities. Purchase one with a gazetteer of streets.

MEDIA

Newspapers and magazines. Toronto has four thriving dailies, *The Globe and Mail, The Sun, The Toronto Star*, and *The National Post. Now* and *Eye* are free arts and entertainment weeklies. *Toronto Life* is the major monthly city magazine and *Where Toronto* is usually provided free in your hotel room. At most news-stands, you can purchase a wide variety of international dailies, weeklies, and monthly magazines. The best newsstands are those operated by Great Canadian News Company and Lichtman's, plus the Maison de la Presse Internationale. In better hotels, room ser-vice delivers the paper of your choice along with breakfast.

Radio and television. One of the great jewels of Canada is the *Canadian Broadcasting Company* (CBC), which puts out a mix of music, talk, drama, and news. In Toronto, at 740AM or 99.1FM. CHIN at 1540AM and 100.7FM will get you in touch with the city's multicultural scene. You can find popular music stations on 96.1, 102.1, and 107.1FM.

Every hotel room has a TV (B&Bs often don't) with a choice of network and cable channels. The main network channels are: the CBC, plus American network affiliates CBC, ABC, NBC, and PBS (Public Broadcasting Service). The most useful cable channels are CNN (Cable News Network) for non-stop news, the Weather Chan-nel for national and local forecasts, MuchMusic (MTV), and ESPN for sports. Channel numbers vary.

MONEY

Currency. The Canadian dollar is divided into 100 cents (¢).
Bank notes: C$5, C$20, C$50, C$100.
Coins: 1¢ (penny), 5¢ (nickel), 10¢ (dime), 25¢ (quarter), C$1 (a loonie), C$2 (a toonie).

ATMs. The easiest and often the least expensive way to obtain money abroad is from an ATM (cash machine) with your debit or credit card.

Exchange facilities. Cash and travelers checks can be changed at banks. If you bring travelers checks, make sure to get them in Canadian dollar denominations – they're hard to exchange otherwise. **Credit cards**. Debit cards are accepted in most stores and restaurants. **Travelers checks**. Banks will exchange Canadian-denomination travelers checks for cash without charge (take ID with you). Most places accept them as payment and C$20 checks are the most useful. **Tax**. Advertised prices do not include tax. An 8 percent provincial sales tax is added to the purchase price of most goods, including hotel and restaurant checks. In addition, a 5 percent federal sales tax applies to all goods and services (GST) bought in Canada. Visitors may claim a partial rebate of this tax by acquiring a form at customs on leaving Canada. For information, contact Revenue Canada, tel: (902) 432-5604 or 1 (800) 565-9353.

O

OPENING HOURS

Banks are generally open Monday to Thursday 9am–5pm and Friday 9am–6pm. Stores open Monday to Wednesday 10am–6pm and Saturday and Sunday 10am–5pm. Hours are often extended on Thursday and Friday until 8 or 9pm. The subway stops running at 1.30am.

P

POLICE

In an emergency, dial **911**. Downtown, call (416) 808-5200 for non-emergency police matters, such as reporting a theft.

POST OFFICES

The Canadian Post Office's hours are generally 8am–5.45pm, Monday to Saturday, although postal franchises in drugstores and small businesses often stay open longer. There are two main post offices with

Saturday hours: Atrium on Bay at 595 Bay Street, 10am–6pm, and First Canadian Place at 100 King Street West, 10am–5pm.

Stamps are sold at post offices, hotel desks, drugstores, and other small shops with a Canada Post emblem. Mailboxes are red and conveniently located on or near street corners. Postcard rates are the same for the US and Canada, but letters are more expensive.

PUBLIC TRANSPORTATION

Bus and subway. The Toronto Transit Commission (TTC) provides efficient service around town via a network of interconnected subway, bus, and streetcar routes. The efficient, safe, and clean subway (underground) is renowned; it covers the city in a north–south loop, with extensions east and west. A light rapid transit system connects downtown to Harbourfront. The subway operates daily from 6am–1.30am (Sunday from 9am). Between 1am and 5.30am a surface network operates on certain routes every 30-minutes. Call (416) 393-4636 for subway and bus info.

Buses and streetcars link up with the subway. Always pick up a transfer, allowing you to change for free between subway and bus and vice-versa. Buses accept only exact fare, transit token, or ticket-transfer bought in train stations. The Queen, Dundas College, and St Clair streetcars and some buses run 24 hours a day.

Ferry service. Ferries operate year-round to the Toronto Islands. Call (416) 392-8193 for information.

Taxis are available at taxi stands near hotels, important concourses, and train stations, and can be hailed in the street or ordered by phone. Try Diamond Taxi (tel: 416/366-6868), Beck Taxi (tel: 416/751-5555), Arrow Taxi and Yellow Cab (tel: 416/504-4141).

Trains. GO (Government of Ontario) Transit services connect Toronto's Union Station with the outer suburbs, as far as Hamilton; tel: (416) 869-3200. Buses also operate in the suburbs.

VIA Rail operates all over Canada. The Toronto terminal is Union Station at Bay and Front streets; tel: 1-888-842-7245.

R

RELIGION

Almost every type of religion and religious sect is represented in Toronto. Roman Catholics and Protestants hold a clear majority, but there is also a diversity of temples. Your hotel desk and the weekend newspapers can help you find out addresses and times of services.

T

TELEPHONE

There are now two area codes for Toronto. The original 416 still operates, but 647 is being introduced. For all local calls, the area code must be dialled followed by the telephone number. The area code 905 is for the surrounding 'greater Toronto.'

Dial 0 for the operator, 411 for local information, 1-555-1212 for long distance information, and 011 plus the country code and phone number for an international call.

TICKETS

Tickets can be purchased at theater box offices or by credit card via TicketMaster (tel: 416/870-8000 <www.ticketmaster.ca>). Half-price tickets are available at the T.O. Tix booth at Yonge Dundas Square; open Tuesday through Saturday noon–7.30pm. For information, call (416) 536-6468.

For tickets to Toronto Blue Jays games call (416) 341-1234.

TIME ZONES

Toronto and most of Ontario is on Eastern Time, the same as New York and the entire US East Coast, which is five hours behind Greenwich Mean Time. The second Sunday in March marks the start of Daylight Saving Time, when clocks are advanced one hour.

Clocks are turned back one hour at the end of Daylight Saving Time on the first Sunday in November.

Los Angeles	Chicago	**Toronto**	London	Paris
9am	11am	**noon**	5pm	6pm

TIPPING

As in the US, a service charge is not normally included in hotel and restaurant bills, so tipping is customary. You may use your discretion, but here are some guidelines:

Hotel porter, per bag	C$1–2
Maid, per day	C$1–2
Waiter	15 percent
Hairdresser/barber	15 percent
Taxi driver	10–20 percent
Tour guide	15 percent

TOILETS

Torontonians will probably understand you if you ask for the 'bathroom,' 'men's/ladies' room,' 'restroom,' 'washroom,' 'lavatory,' 'loo,' or 'john.' Conveniences are usually clean, and easily found in shopping complexes, filling stations, museums, and cafés and bars. If there's an attendant, leave a tip.

TOURIST INFORMATION

Before you leave. The Ontario Ministry of Tourism (<www.tourism. gov.on.ca>) and the Canadian Government Office of Tourism (<www.canada.worldweb.com>) operate information services in many countries. They can supply a host of brochures and maps covering everything from hotels and transportation to special vacations.
Australia: Consulate General of Canada, Quay West Building, 111 Harrington Street, Level 5, Sydney NSW 2000; tel: (012) 9-364-3000.

New Zealand: Canadian High Commission, Level 11, 125 The Terrace, Thorndon, Wellington; tel: (644) 473-9577.

South Africa: Canadian High Commission, 1103 Arcadia Street, Hatfield, 0028, Pretoria; tel: (012) 422-3000.

UK: Canadian High Commission, 38 Grosvenor Street, London W1K 4AA; tel: (020) 7258-6600. Information is also available from Canada House in Trafalgar Square, tel: (020) 7569-6600.

US: The Canadian consulates in the US will not provide tourist information. They will only refer you to the offices in Toronto.

In Toronto. Tourism Toronto, Queen's Quay Terminal at Harbourfront, PO Box 126, 207 Queen's Quay West, Suite 590, Toronto, ON, M5J 1A7; tel: (416) 203-2500, (800) 499-2514 (toll-free in the US and Canada, <www.tourismtoronto.com>). It's open Monday to Friday 8.30am–6pm. There's also an information booth just inside the Convention Centre on Front Street.

Ontario. If you require information about Ontario, contact Ontario Travel at 20 Dundas Street West; tel: (416) 314-5899. Open Monday through Saturday 10am–6pm, Sunday noon–5pm.

W

WEBSITES

There are a number of good general-information sites about Toronto that can help you with accommodations, tourist information, and entertainment guides. The best are <www.tourismtoronto.com>, <www.travelinx.com>, and <www.toronto.com>.

To preview the media available in Toronto, go to the sites operated by some of its newspapers. These include:

www.globeandmail.com
www.nationalpost.com
www.nowtoronto.com
www.thestar.ca

Check in also at the CBC's **www.cbc.ca**

Many of Toronto's major attractions and sports teams also have their own websites.

WEIGHTS AND MEASURES

Canada uses the metric system for most measurements. You'll see road signs marked in kilometers, not miles. Weather reports are given in Celsius. Food and clothes may be measured by both the metric and American/British systems.

Y

YOUTH HOSTELS

Toronto has a very good downtown hostel, Toronto Global Village Backpackers, at 460 King Street West; tel: 1-888-344-7875. Also worth a try if you're looking for a place to stay on a limited budget are two websites with booking facilities: <www.hostel world.com> and <www.hostels.com>.

In summer, other great resources for low-cost accommodations are the universities; you can usually stay in dorms (some of them even have private bathrooms) and use the additional university facilities for a very reasonable price.

The best bet for a downtown location in the summertime is Victoria University at 140 Charles Street West (tel: 416/585-4524) or Neil Wycik College Hotel at 96 Gerrard Street East between Church and Jarvis (tel: 416/977-2320 or 1-800-268-4358, <www.neill-wycik.com>). There are also accommodations at the Scarborough campus of the University of Toronto; for information call (416) 287-7356.

Recommended Hotels

There are plenty of fine hotels in Toronto, and they are relatively in-expensive if you compare them to their equivalents in New York or other world capitals. There are very few budget-oriented hotels, how-ever. Your best bet for low-cost accommodations are B&Bs, youth hostels, and, during student holidays, campus dorm accommodations. Before making your plans, ask your travel agent about airline and other tour packages, which can sometimes deliver great savings. Prices are highest from 1 April through 30 November and lowest from December to February.

Listed below is a selection of hotels in four price categories. As a basic guide we have used the symbols below to indicate prices for a double room with bath, not including the 5 percent accommodations tax or the 7 percent GST (see tax refund information on page 118). All take major credit cards unless otherwise noted.

$$$$	C$300 and above
$$$	C$226–C$300
$$	C$151–C$225
$	C$150 and under

DOWNTOWN

Best Western Primrose Hotel $ *111 Carlton Street (between Church and Jarvis), M5B 2G3, tel: (416) 977-8000 or 1-800-268-8082 (toll-free in the US and Canada), fax: (416) 977-6323, <www.bestwestern.com>.* Large, comfortable rooms with standard equip-ment, hairdryer, and coffeemaker. Café and lounge. Facilities include business center, outdoor pool, and exercise room. 350 rooms.

Bond Place Hotel $–$$ *65 Dundas Street East, M5B 2G8, tel: (416) 362-6061 or 1-800-268-9390, fax: (416) 360-6406, <www.bondplacehoteltoronto.com>.* A mid-sized hotel in a good down-town location one block from the shopping Mecca, Eaton Centre. Rooms at reasonable prices. The decor is dated but clean enough. Café and lounge. 286 rooms.

Cambridge Suites Hotel $$$$ *15 Richmond Street East, M5C 1N2, tel: (416) 368-1990 or 1-800-463-1990, fax: (416) 601-3751, <www.cambridgesuitestoronto.com>.* An exclusive all-suite hotel in the financial district that caters to business people. Each suite is equipped with microwave, refrigerator, coffeemaker, two televisions, fax, and two dual-line phones with data port. Fitness center, restaurant, and bar. Complimentary in-suite breakfast. No phone access charges. 229 suites.

Cosmopolitan $$$$ *8 Colborne Street (just off Yonge), M5E 1E1, tel: (416) 350-2000 or 1-800-958-3488, fax: (416) 350-2460, <www.cosmotoronto.com>.* A boutique hotel with zen flair: complimentary incense sticks and semi-precious healing stones and feng shui decor; air purifiers, an on-site spa and an Asian fusion restaurant. 97 rooms.

Courtyard Marriott $$–$$$ *475 Yonge Street, M4Y 1X7, tel: (416) 924-0611 or 1-800-847-5075, <www.mariott.com>.* This Marriott opened in late 1999 at Yonge and Carlton, close to downtown. The rooms are attractively furnished and have a hairdryer, coffeemaker, and two phones with data port. Fitness center with lap pool. Restaurant. 575 rooms.

Days Inn and Conference Centre $–$$ *30 Carlton Street, M58 2E9, tel: (416) 977-6655 or 1-800-367-9601 (toll-free in the US and Canada), fax: (416) 977-0502, <www.dayshoteltoronto.ca>.* Near the Yonge Street subway in the heart of the city. Indoor heated pool, sauna and fitness facilities, beauty salon and barber shop. Windows family café, plus The Beer Cellar Bar and Lounge. 538 rooms.

Delta Chelsea Inn $$–$$$ *33 Gerrard Street West, M5G 1Z4, tel: (416) 595-1975 or 1-800-242-5732, fax: (416) 585-4375, <www.deltahotels.com>.* A large hotel attracting business people and families. Babysitting service, children's for 3–12-year-olds, and Starcade for older children. Kitchenettes on request. Business rooms include fax, printer, phone and internet connection. Two restaurants, four lounges. Adult-only fitness center, plus a family pool. 1,590 rooms.

The Drake Hotel $$–$$$ *1150 Queen Street West, M6J 1J3, tel: (416) 531-5042 or (866) DRAKE-TO (toll-free in the US and Canada), fax: (416) 350-3155, <www.thedrakehotel.ca>.* In 2006 *Travel and Leisure* magazine named The Drake one of the 500 best hotels in the world. It's a vintage hotel saved from decay and renovated to provide chic boutique accommodation. Small rooms with antique furniture and windows that can open. One of the arts scene's hottest nightspots downstairs, guests can eat, drink and people-watch in the bars, lounge and cafés. 19 rooms.

Fairmont Royal York $$$–$$$$ *100 Front Street West, M5J 1E3, tel: (416) 368-2511 or 1-800-441-1414, fax: (416) 368-9040, <www.fairmont.com>.* A massive institution that has catered to many legendary names and events since it opened its doors in 1929. For some, the size is so overpowering that it detracts from the service – 2,800 guests can sleep here. The rooms have been refurbished and are appropriately furnished with antique reproductions. There are three restaurants, including Epic, the premier dining room, and three lounges; 24-hour room service. Indoor pool and fitness center. Business center. 1,365 rooms.

The Gladstone Hotel $$ *1214 Queen Street West M6J 1J6, tel: (416) 531-4635, fax: (416) 539-0953, <www.gladstonehotel.com>.* Art hotels are an international trend, and The Gladstone is Toronto's own. The city's oldest operating hotel was formerly down-at-heel; now it maintains its popularity with events for the local art, music and literary crowds while attracting guests to its eclectic artist-designed suites. 37 rooms.

Hôtel Le Germain Toronto $$–$$$ *30 Mercer Street, M5V 1H3, tel: (416) 345-9500 or 1-866-345-9501 (toll-free in the US and Canada), fax: (416) 345-9501, <www.germaintoronto.com>.* This stylish and welcoming boutique hotel is part of the family-owned Groupe Germain, which has three successful boutique hotels elsewhere in Canada, in Montréal, Québec and Old Québec. Situated in the entertainment district, just a stone's throw from the CN Tower, the hotel has a sleek, modernist design, its decor and furnishings a discreet blend of minimalism and elegance. 122 rooms.

Hotel Victoria $ *56 Yonge Street (at Wellington), M5E 1G5, tel: (416) 363-1666 or 1-800-363-8228, fax: (416) 363-7327, <www.hotel victoria-toronto.com>.* A small hotel in a landmark building in the financial district. It has standard (slightly smaller) rooms equipped with typical comforts plus deluxe rooms with such amenities as coffeemaker and refrigerator. There's also a restaurant and bar, and access to a nearby health club. 56 rooms.

Intercontinental Toronto Centre $$$ *225 Front Street West, M5V 2X3, tel: (416) 597-1400 or 1-800-422-7969, fax: (416) 597-8128, <www.torontocentre.intercontinental.com>.* Conveniently located next to the Convention Centre and close to all the downtown tourist stops. The rooms at this hotel are elegantly decorated and well equipped. Azure, the premier restaurant, serves delicious food and deserves accolades. The Victoria Spa has 12 treatment rooms, a juice bar, whirlpool, and saunas. Indoor pool, fitness facilities, and sun-deck. 587 rooms.

Le Royal Meridien King Edward Hotel $$–$$$ *37 King Street, East M5C 1E9, tel: (416) 863-9700 or 1-800-545-4300, fax: (416) 367-5515, <www.lemeridien-kingedward.com>.* Built in 1903, this is Toronto's oldest and most beloved hotel. The lobby's marble columns and glass-domed rotunda provide a grand welcome. It's a lovely place to take a traditional English tea. The rooms are decorated with plush fabrics and furnishings and have every amenity. One restaurant and bar. 24-hour room service. Facilities include business center, exercise room, and spa. 296 rooms.

The Metropolitan Hotel $$–$$$ *108 Chestnut Street, M5G 1R3, tel: (416) 977-5000 or 1-800-668-6600, fax: (416) 977-9513, <www.metropolitan.com>.* An upmarket hotel catering to a business crowd. The rooms have large desks and such added comforts as bathrobes and massage showerheads, plus a safe and ISDN lines. The Hemispheres restaurant has an eclectic and innovative menu and extensive wine list, while the Lai Wah Heen serves some of the best and most authentic Cantonese cuisine outside of Hong Kong. Try the dim sum if you can. Indoor swimming pool; fitness center with massage. 422 rooms.

Neill Wycik College Hotel $ *96 Gerrard Street East (between Church and Jarvis), M5B 1G7, tel: (416) 977-2320 or 1-800-268-4358, fax: (416) 977-2809, <www.neill-wycik.com>.* Clean, modern, and inexpensive. Used by students in term times, this hotel rents apartment-style units containing four or five bedrooms that share two bathrooms and a kitchen. Each room can accommodate anywhere from one to five beds. Rooms have telephones but no air-conditioning. Facilities include TV lounge, sauna, café, and rooftop sundeck. May through August only. 300 rooms.

Novotel $$ *45 The Esplanade, M5E 1W2, tel: (416) 367-8900 or 1-800-668-6835, fax: (416) 360-8285, <www.novotel.com>.* A modern hotel built in neo-French Renaissance style around the corner from the Hummingbird Centre and within walking distance of the Financial District. Rooms are well-equipped (telephones, minibar, and hairdryer). Fitness center, indoor pool. Restaurant and lounge. 262 rooms.

Radisson Plaza Hotel Admiral $$$ *249 Queen's Quay West, M5J 2N5, tel: (416) 203-3333 or 1-800-201-1718, fax: (416) 203-3100, <www.radisson.com/torontoca_admiral>.* Located right on the harbor. The lobby and restaurant, bar, and café have a nautical theme achieved with brass and polished wood. It has the best sundeck, cabaña-style bar, and outdoor pool in the city. Beautiful rooms come with all the amenities – two telephones, hairdryer, and coffeemaker. 24-hour room service. 157 rooms.

Ramada Plaza Toronto $$ *300 Jarvis Street, M5B 2C5, tel: (416) 977-4823 or 1-800-567-2233, fax: (416) 977-4830, <www.ramadaplazatoronto.com>.* Located in a slightly dicey neighborhood, this is a favorite for tour groups. It offers many amenities for such a moderately priced hotel – refrigerators, hairdryers, coffeemakers. Indoor pool, fitness center, squash courts. Bistro and bar. 102 rooms.

Renaissance Toronto Hotel at Rogers Centre $$–$$$ *1 Blue Jays Way, M5V 1J4, tel: (416) 341-7100 or 1-800-237-1512, fax: (416) 341-5091.* Located in the heart of the city's entertainment district, next to the Metro Toronto Convention Centre and the CN Tower, this renovated and very flash hotel is actually attached to Rogers Centre, with 70 of its rooms overlooking the stadium floor. Guests have access to comprehensive state-of-the-art leisure and business facilities. 346 rooms.

The Sheraton Centre $$$ *123 Queen Street West, M5H 2M9, tel: (416) 361-1000 or 1-866-716-8101 (toll-free in the US and Canada), fax: (416) 947-4854, <www.sheratoncentretoronto.com>.* A favorite stopover with business people. It is a large, modern convention hotel overlooking City Hall and connected to the underground mall. Well-equipped rooms; special amenities. Rapid response is the hallmark; in the café, if breakfast isn't delivered in five minutes it's free. Three restaurants, two lounges. Indoor/outdoor pool, sun deck, fitness center, and business center. It's also child-friendly (supervised play area for kids 18 months to 12 years). 1,377 rooms.

The SoHo Metropolitan $$$–$$$$ *318 Wellington Street West, M5V 1T4, tel: (416) 599-8800 or 1-866-SOHO-MET (toll-free in the US and Canada), fax: (416) 599-8801, <www.sohomet.com>.* With its curving glass facades, this was Toronto's first boutique hotel. The 'luxury lifestyle' complex includes the upscale Senses restaurant, a café, bar, athletic club, and spa. Located in the hub of the theater and entertainment district, rooms in the upper floors offer a stunning view of the Toronto skyline. 86 rooms.

The Strathcona Hotel $–$$ *60 York Street, M5J 1S8, tel: (416) 363-3321 or 1-800-268-8304, fax: (416) 363-4679, <www.the strathconahotel.com>.* You can't beat the price or the location, right across from the Fairmont Royal York. The rooms are modern and equipped with TV and telephone and there's a restaurant, lounge, and tavern. 194 rooms.

Toronto International Hostel $ *76 Church Street north of King, M5C 2G1, tel: (416) 971-4440 or 1-877-848-8737 (toll-free in the US and Canada), fax: (416) 971-4088, <www.hihostels.ca>.* A good deal right downtown. Typical dorm accommodations with anywhere from four to 10 beds. Air-conditioned, each dorm has a bathroom.

There are also a few double rooms available with private bathroom. Facilities include kitchen, laundry, and TV lounge. 170 beds.

Westin Harbour Castle $$$ *1 Harbour Square, M5J 1A6, tel: (416) 869-1600 or 1-800-937-8461, fax: (416) 869-0573, <www.starwood hotels.com/westin>*. Large, comfortable hotel on the lakeshore; almost half of the rooms have lake views. The rooms have recently been redecorated and feature two telephones with data ports. Toula is the hotel's Italian restaurant and there is also a bar. Facilities include indoor pool, two squash courts, and outdoor tennis. 24-hour room service. 977 rooms.

MIDTOWN

The Four Seasons $$$$ *21 Avenue Road, M5R 2G1, tel: (416) 964-0411 or 1-800-819-5053 (toll-free in the US and Canada), fax: (416) 964-2301, <www.fourseasons.com>*. Located in Yorkville, this is the city's premier hotel, providing the ultimate in service and comfort. Huge, exquisitely furnished rooms with every conceivable amenity. Facilities include health club, indoor/outdoor pool, 24-hour room service, and concierge. One-hour pressing. Truffles restaurant is top-notch. One bar and a handsome café too. Children welcome, with bicycles, supervised play center, and more. 380 rooms.

Hotel Intercontinental $$$$ *220 Bloor Street West, M5S 1T8, tel: (416) 960-5200 or 1-888-424-6835 (toll-free in the US and Canada), fax: (416) 960-8269, <www.toronto.intercontinental. com>*. Comfort and personal service are the hallmarks of this small hotel in Yorkville. Spacious rooms are nicely furnished and equipped with dual line phones with data port, a safe, iron/ironing board, plus additional amenities in business rooms. Restaurant, lounge with fireplace, and lovely courtyard in summer. Rooftop sundeck, indoor lap pool, and fitness center. Business center. Good Kids in Tow program. 24-hour room service. 210 rooms.

Park Hyatt Toronto $$$ *4 Avenue Road, M5R 2E8, tel: (416) 925-1234, fax: (416) 924-4933, <www.parktoronto.hyatt.com>*. This hotel in Yorkville, across from the Four Seasons, has completed a

$60-million renovation, redecorating the rooms in fine fabrics and furnishings and adding the latest in amenities – dual-line phones with data port, fax, and more. The lounge is famous for the literary lights that have gathered around the hearth. Large fitness center and spa. 24-hour room service and concierge. 346 rooms.

Victoria University $ *140 Charles Street West, M5S 1K9, tel: (416) 585-4524, fax: (416) 585-4530, <www.vicu.utoronto.ca/facilities/ accommodations.htm>*. Located directly across from the Royal Ontario Museum. Rooms available from mid-May to late August only, are small but adequate, with bathrooms down the hall. Breakfast included. 800 rooms.

Windsor Arms $$$$ *18 St Thomas Street, M5S 3E7, tel: (416) 971-9666, fax: (416) 921-9121, <www.windsorarmshotel.com>*. This wonderful landmark hotel was revived in the 1990s. Located just off Bloor Street, it has super-luxury amenities in its suites. Frette linens and rich fabrics and furnishings adorn the rooms. The bathrooms have whirlpool and separate shower. The suites are also equipped with the ultimate technology – DVD, fax, and three dual-line phones with data port plus a portable. The Courtyard Café is as beautiful as ever; caviar and champagne lounge too. Spa with pool. 26 suites and two standard rooms.

UPTOWN

Best Western Roehampton Hotel $$ *808 Mount Pleasant Road, M4P 2L2, tel: (416) 487-5101 or 1-800-387-8899, fax: (416) 487 5390, <www.bestwestern.com>*. This hotel has large rooms with refrigerators for a fairly reasonable price. Restaurant, exercise room, outdoor rooftop pool, and sundeck. 109 rooms.

Montecassino Hotel $$ *3710 Chesswood Drive, M3J 2W4, tel: (416) 630-8100, or 1-800-334-8774, fax: (416) 630-1929, <www.montecassino.on.ca>*. An affordable, modern, three-star hotel. Near the corporate district and Canada's Wonderland theme park. Rooms sleep up to four; children under 12 stay free. Access to fitness club. Transportation to the airport and city. 104 rooms.

Recommended Restaurants

Toronto is a great city for dining. Explore the diverse neighborhoods – Greektown on the Danforth in the East End; the main Chinatown along Dundas and Spadina; and Little Italy along College Street. Here you'll find ethnic restaurants serving good food at reasonable prices.

The restaurants listed are categorized by neighborhood, and by price in Canadian dollars per person for a three-course meal:

$$$$	C$45 and above
$$$	C$35–C$45
$$	C$25–C$35
$	C$25 and under

DOWNTOWN WEST

Barberian's Steak House $$$$ *7 Elm Street, tel: (416) 597-0335.* Lunch Mon–Fri; dinner daily. A favorite Toronto steakhouse. Decorated with Canadiana, it attracts a traditional crowd who appreciates the 10 different cuts that are grilled to perfection. Excellent, varied wine list.

Bar Italia $$ *582 College Street West, tel: (416) 535-3621.* Lunch and dinner daily; brunch Sat–Sun. Situated in the heart of Little Italy, this sleekly modern restaurant has comfy banquettes and a people-watching street-front patio. Authentic Italian fare is hearty and in-expensive, and upstairs a dimly lit lounge offers live jazz in fall and winter months. Grilled calamari, a well-edited wine list and the modernist interior make this a popular spot on the College stretch.

The Beaconsfield $$ *1154 Queen Street West, tel: (416) 516-2550.* Dinner daily. This beautifully restored bar and bistro with scarlet leather banquettes and period lighting is situated in the heart of the Queen Street West gallery district, and is a favourite among the art crowd. The delectable menu offers everything from truffle crusted beef carpacio, to an elevated twist on the French Canadian classic poutine (made here with hand cut frites in veal jus with Canadian cheese curd).

Canoe $$$ *66 Wellington Street West, tel: (416) 364-0054.* Lunch and dinner Mon–Fri. On the 54th floor of the Toronto Dominion Bank tower, this sophisticated restaurant caters to the business crowd. The place to go for traditional Canadian fare (Digby scallops, Alberta beef, Yukon caribou, Ontario pheasant) prepared in creative ways. Great views of the surrounding skyline.

Chiado $$$ *864 College Street (at Concord), tel: (416) 538-1910.* Lunch Mon–Fri; dinner daily. An elegant Lisbon-style restaurant named after the city's old quarter, that offers some fine traditional fresh fish dishes, including *pinheta* of salt cod and many other Portuguese specialties.

Czehoski $$$ *678 Queen Street West, tel: (416) 366-6787.* Lunch Tue–Fri; dinner daily; brunch Sat–Sun. By keeping the wooden butcher's block and faded painted sign out front, this stylish eatery pays homage to the 1920s Polish butcher shop that once thrived here. Now a hip gathering place for late night drinks and original fare, Chef Nathan Isberg describes his style as 'decadent comfort food' and that it is. Main courses include brie and truffle pierogies, and hen 'cooked under heavy things' with spaetzle and swiss chard truffled chicken jus.

Foxley Bistro $$$ *207 Ossington Avenue, tel: (416) 534-8520.* Dinner Mon–Sat. This low-key bistro located in the revived Ossington strip is the brainchild of ex-Tempo chef Tom Tai, previously known for his delectably modern take on sushi. Here the menu includes an eclectic assortment of Asian-influenced South American and Latin flavors. The sea bream ceviche with yuzu and shiso leaf, and the spring rolls of grilled portabello mushroom, chipotle, vine leaf and herb salad, are two of the many reasons why this small restaurant is on food critics' radars.

Golden Turtle $ *125 Ossington Avenue, tel: (416) 531-1601.* Lunch and dinner daily. This non-descript looking fixture on the corner of Ossington and Argyle streets, is where Toronto's culinary darling, Susur Lee has been spotted slurping the Vietnamese noodle-house's now well known pho (a classic soup of thinly sliced rare beef atop rice noodles in rich broth with sweet spices). The seafood pho is comprised of sweet chicken stock with al dente egg vermicelli, barely wilted leaf lettuce, and mixed seafood, including big shrimp and fish balls. With some pho soups priced at less than $5, this is one of the best culinary deals in town.

Julie's Cuban $$ *202 Dovercourt Road, tel: (416) 532-7397.* Dinner Tue–Sun. A varied tapas menu, including calamari and fried plantains, plus the cozy Cuban-style atmosphere nestled in a residential tree-lined street, makes this *boîte* a local favorite.

Café La Gaffe $$ *24 Baldwin Street, tel: (416) 596-2397.* Lunch Mon–Fri; dinner Mon–Sat. A popular French bistro with outdoor terrace. The setting is comfortable French with wooden banquettes; the food is good bistro-style fare (steak frites, *chêvre* salad and thin-crust pizza), and there is an extensive list of rare wines from which to choose.

Lai Wah Heen $$$ *108 Chestnut Street (in the Metropolitan Hotel), tel: (416) 977-9899.* Lunch and dinner daily. An authentic Hong Kong-style Chinese restaurant that serves haute Cantonese and some of the best dim sum (40 selections) in the city, in a spare and elegant dining room with only a bit of calligraphy for decoration. There are 20 shark's fin and abalone selections, plus many more exotic specialties for guests to try.

Lee $$$ *603 King Street West, tel: (416) 504-7867.* Dinner Mon–Sat. Next door to his eponymous eatery, Susur Lee's bistro offers a wide variety of smaller dishes that are Asian-inspired and affordable. Lee also has combo dinners for C$25 – great value considering his food has an international reputation.

Lee Garden $ *331 Spadina Avenue, tel: (416) 593-9524.* Dinner daily. Chinese restaurant that specializes in seafood: fresh oysters, abalone, shrimp and pineapple, and steamed cod with black-bean sauce. Excellent and inexpensive. No reservations.

MataHari Bar and Grill $ *39 Baldwin Street, tel: (416) 596-2832.* Lunch Tue–Fri; dinner Tue–Sun. Tamarind, lemongrass, chili, coconut curry are some of the flavors and spices in the cuisine at this Malaysian spot. Small, comfortable dining room offering great value.

La Palette $$–$$$ *256 Augusta, tel: (416) 929-4900.* Dinner daily. A romantic French bistro with excellent authentic French fare and a sophisticated wine list (sampling is encouraged). Three- course *prix fixe* is a reasonable C$25.

Rain $$–$$$ *19 Mercer Street, tel: (416) 599-7246.* Dinner Tue–Sat. Award-winning design firm II by IV transformed what was previously a women's prison into an Asian-inspired space. A large waterfall graces one side with an underlit bar and oversized round couch. An upright bamboo screen divides the lounge area from the dining section where 30-something patrons consume exquisite fare at a long, communal table.

Rodney's Oyster House $$ *469 King Street West, tel: (416) 363-8105.* Lunch and dinner Mon–Sat. This acclaimed source for oysters in Toronto moved into this larger space below grade at King and Spadina. Chain link, corrugated metal and chipboard contribute to the down-home East Coast ambiance. The selection of oysters on the half shell is the best in the city, with fish, shrimp, and lobster also on the menu.

San $ *676 Queen Street West, tel: (416) 214-9429.* Dinner Tue–Sat; lunch Tue–Sun. Walls washed with a soft green light, and cool tunes spin in this Korean-Japanese restaurant that looks as though the prices should be higher than they are. *Bee bim bap*, a mix of spicy vegetables, meat and rice is served in hot, stone bowls. Bento boxes make a complete meal with sushi, noodles, salad, and soup. An extensive saki list and Japanese beers.

Saving Grace $ *907 Dundas Street West, tel: (416) 703-7368.* Mon–Fri 9am–3pm (closed Wed), Sat–Sun 10am–3pm. This minimalist but cozy neighborhood boîte is one of the few places in town to offer a delicious weekday brunch. Local film and music celebrities are often seen sipping coffee here, but the main draw is the daily specials, including their 'eggs of the moment' which can be everything from Indian to South American inspired. Their homemade granola is exceptional, as is their take on French toast: a crispy French baguette served with caramelized bananas and organic maple syrup.

Siddhartha $ *647A King Street West at Bathurst, tel: (416) 703-6684 and 1450 Gerrard Street East, tel: (416) 465-4095.* King: 1–2.30pm and 5.30–9.30pm daily; Gerrard: noon–10pm daily. Clean and friendly Indian eatery that's equally popular in its downtown location as in its original venue in Gerrard Indian Bazaar. All dishes are tasty, but the buffet (with items at moderate and pungent spice levels) is what keeps diners coming back for more.

Susur $$$–$$$$ *601 King Street West, tel: (416) 603-2205.* Dinner Mon–Sat. Touted by *Food & Wine* as one of the world's 10 most important chefs, Susur Lee collaborated with his wife Brenda Bent and architect Greg Colucci on the serene design of this wonderful 70-seat restaurant. Dishes such as spiced venison with mountain potatoes and *uni* are reflective of Lee's diverse culinary roots, not to mention elevating food to an art form.

Swan $$ *790 Queen Street West, tel: (416) 532-0452.* Lunch and dinner daily. Art deco banquettes, a Formica counter and a retro Coca-Cola cooler filled with oysters create a diner-with-attitude feel. Bistro fare includes a daily mussels special, oyster concoctions, and delicious desserts.

Taro Grill $$ *492 Queen Street West, tel: (416) 504-1320.* Lunch and dinner daily. Taro Grill is a very hip spot serving pastas and pizzas, and such dishes as Asian-style barbecue chicken (in a teriyaki garlic sauce) and rack of lamb with a rosemary merlot glaze. Good value place.

Terroni $$ *720 Queen Street West, tel: (416) 504-0320.* Lunch and dinner daily. Tasty traditional southern Italian fare has been served up in the Queen Street stalwart since 1992; several more branches have emerged in other locations throughout the city. A line snakes out the door most nights, but it moves quickly and allows for some of the best people-watching while you wait. Purists with their thin crust wood-fired pizzas, Terroni refuses to cut them into slices – all pizzas are served whole. Spicy Penne Arrabiata and baked oyster mushroom Funghi Assoluti are beloved standbys.

Utopia $ *586 College Street, tel: (416) 534-7751.* Lunch and dinner daily. This mainstay of the College Street strip owes its success to its laid-back atmosphere and ample, globe-trotting menu: there is something for everyone here. In the summertime the large sun-filled patio is the perfect place to stop for a cold drink and one of their famous burger or quesadilla plates. The wine list includes many Ontario vintages and beers from local microbreweries are on tap.

Xacutti $$$ *503 College Street, tel: (416) 323-3957.* Dinner Tue–Sun; brunch Sat–Sun. An impossibly stylish interior complete with chocolate banquettes and giant Ingo Maurer fixtures, Xacutti (pronounced 'sha-koo-tee') caters to Toronto's design cognoscenti. An Indian-inspired cuisine features delectable dishes including saffron snapper in coconut lime curry and pan-fried jeera halibut.

DOWNTOWN EAST

Colborne Lane $$$ *45 Colborne Street, tel: (416) 368-9009.* Lunch Mon–Fri; dinner Mon–Sat. Open since the winter of 2006, chef Claudio Aprile has wowed diners with his rich, complex, modern cooking. Dishes such as his licorice and burnt honey sauce on tender Peking duck, and hibiscus and salt-cured foie gras have garnered outstanding reviews and make reservations in this well-appointed restaurant essential.

Gio Rana's Really Really Nice Italian Restaurant $$$ *1220 Queen Street East at Leslie, tel: (416) 469-5225.* Tue–Sat 6–11pm. Gio is so well known and his places so popular with locals that he rarely even hangs a sign; this one only has a huge sculpture of a nose hanging over the door. The homey, creative, Italian-inspired menu includes side dishes that can be shared. Every night is a convivial party packed with east-end foodies who've discovered the growing Queen Street East dining strip.

Jamie Kennedy Wine Bar $$$ *9 Church Street, tel: (416) 362-5586.* Lunch and dinner daily. Top Toronto chef Jamie Kennedy has created a sumptuous menu consisting of tasting dishes (such as PEI mussels, Swedish meatballs, and acclaimed Yukon Gold frites) paired with suggested wines from the extensive list of new and old world vintages.

Jump Café and Bar $$$ *Commerce Court East, 18 Wellington Street West, tel: (416) 363-3400.* Lunch and dinner Mon–Sat. Designed by Robert Meiklejohn, this airy, contemporary bistro has been successfully catering to the pinstripe-suit crowd for over 10 years.

Kaiseki-Sakura $$–$$$ *556 Church Street, tel: (416) 923-1010.* With it's sleek black banquettes and pink back-lit bar it could be mistaken for a modern lounge, but the restaurant has been touted as the best sushi restaurant in town. With elaborate Japanese tasting menus and intricate courses such as deboned quail topped with 'sea foie gras' (monkfish liver), soy and miso-soaked mushrooms and tofu, with a side of tiny water chestnut chips.

Lucien $$–$$$ *36 Wellington Street East, tel: (416) 504-9990.* Dinner Mon–Sat. An eclectic but elegant room is the ideal backdrop for the contemporary, and technically-masterful food of chef Scot Woods. A signature Woods dish is deconstructed southern fried chicken: he removes the skin, cooks the meat, fries the skin crispy and 'glues' it back onto breast meat with buttermilk. Hot, enriched buttermilk encircles a small round croquette. On the side are lightly creamed collards, smooth onion gravy and buttermilk foam.

Nami Japanese Seafood $$$–$$$$ *55 Adelaide Street East, tel: (416) 362-7373.* Lunch Mon–Fri; dinner Mon–Sat. Very chic sushi and sashimi restaurant that caters to business people. Carefully prepared sushi plus robata bar. Try the beef sashimi – thinly sliced beef with a ponzu sauce.

Perigée $$$$ *Cannery Building, 2nd floor, Distillery Historic District, 55 Mill Street, tel: (416) 364-1397, <www.perigeerestaurant.com>.* Seatings every half hour by reservation only; Tue–Sat

5.30–9pm. Chef Pat Riley has turned a tiny upper room into one of the city's most intimate dining experiences: patrons in the room's 36 seats watch their meal being prepared in an open kitchen. Sensational, informed service; tasting menus only; wonderful wines. The chef even takes diners allergies into account when preparing the food. A four-course dessert tasting can be arranged after 9.30pm at around $40 per person.

Rashnaa $ *307 Wellesley Street East, tel: (416) 929-2099.* Lunch and dinner daily. What looks like a nondescript house in Cabbagetown, actually serves-up some of the finest south Indian and Sri Lankan curries in Toronto. The *thosa* are stuffed with spicy chicken, pork, or beef, tandoori butter chicken is flavorful and fried roti bread is the perfect thing for sopping up sweet, spicy curries.

Rectory Café $–$$ *102 Lakeshore Boulevard, Ward's Island, tel: (416) 203-2152, <www.therectorycafe.com>.* Winter Wed–Sun 11am–5pm, summer daily 11am–8pm or later. A unique experience: soup and sandwich lunches or unhurried dinners with a leisurely bottle of wine in a converted rectory, which is perched on the boardwalk overlooking the lake and the tranquil island parkland. Fish and lamb dishes are praiseworthy, as is their elegant take on grilled cheese sandwiches with wholegrain and *chèvre*. The only place to eat on the island.

Shopsy's $ *33 Yonge Street, tel: (416) 365-3333.* Breakfast, lunch, and dinner daily. This establishment has moved since its opening in 1925, but it remains a city institution and the best deli in Toronto. It has long catered to the theater crowd that steadily trickles in at night. They offer a great breakfast, too.

Toast $$ *993 Queen Street East, tel: (416) 778-7299.* Lunch and dinner Tue–Fri; brunch Sat–Sun 10am–4pm. Exposed brick, 1950s-style tables and chairs create a relaxed backdrop for this crowded brunch spot. Everything from cinnamon french toast to eggs florentine can be found on the restaurant's delectable brunch menu. The work of local artists is displayed in the dining room.

MIDTOWN

93 Harbord $$–$$$ *93 Harbord Street, tel: (416) 922-5914.* Dinner Tue–Sun. This understated Annex restaurant offers North African and Middle Eastern-influenced dishes such as slow-braised lamb chops, seared organic chicken breast, and minty bulgur with baby beets and mint chutney.

Boba $$$ *90 Avenue Road, tel: (416) 961-2622.* Dinner Mon–Sat. A sunny Mediterranean ambience warms this fusion restaurant. Well-prepared cuisine with pleasing flavors, like rack of lamb with black olive sauce and potato/fennel gratin. Terrific desserts, including the chocolate-orange crème brûlée.

The Host Fine Indian Cuisine $ *14 Prince Arthur Avenue, tel: (416) 962-4678.* Lunch Mon–Sat; dinner daily. An elegant Indian restaurant serving excellent, fragrant cuisine. Luncheon buffet is popular.

Imperia $–$$ *17A Yorkville Avenue, tel: (416) 921-1471.* Lunch and dinner daily. Simple to high-end Italian dishes are offered here. The thin crust pizza is impeccable, homemade pasta cooked to perfection, and specialties such as lobster risotto are unadulterated Italiana. There is a sturdy wine list, largely of Italian reds, or you can bring your own bottle and pay the corkage fee.

Le Paradis $$ *166 Bedford Road, tel: (416) 921-0995.* Lunch Tue–Fri; dinner daily. An authentic French bistro tucked away from the eastern edge of the design district, Le Paradis serves everything from classic steak frites to rabbit braised with fennel, tomato, and olives, and Moroccan braised lamb shoulder with couscous. The signature homemade fruit tarts never disappoint, and the wine list, along with their menu, has an abundance of inexpensive options.

Live $–$$ *264 Dupont, tel: (416) 515-2002.* Dinner Tue–Sat. This is quite possibly the only restaurant in Toronto without a stove. Chef Jennifer Italiano has created unique vegetarian dishes that are completely raw. Mains include 'rawsagna' and pizza with a sprouted 'crust', and the dessert menu features a selection of 'uncakes'.

Myth $$ *417 Danforth Avenue, tel: (416) 461-8383*. Dinner daily. Dramatic Greek decor and Greek movies shown on TV is a perfect backdrop for Greek/Italian cuisine flavored with garlic, basil, and rosemary. A dozen appetizers (spanakopita, mussels, octopus, and more) precede pizzas, pastas, and such main courses as lemon chicken and lamb brochette.

Oro $$$ *45–47 Elm Street, tel: (416) 597-0155*. Lunch Mon–Fri; dinner Mon–Sat. Modernist Mediterranean food served in this elegant that consistently features in Toronto's 'top ten'. The menu includes seafood minestrone, goat cheese gelato on a tart of caramelized onion and leek in custard, and fork-tender osso bucco.

Ouzeri $ *500a Danforth Avenue, tel: (416) 778-0500*. Lunch and dinner daily. Located on Greek Row (the East End), this is the most popular Greek restaurant along the strip. It serves an array of small dishes (marinated artichokes or octopus) plus such classics as souvlaki and moussaka. No reservations.

Pan on the Danforth $$ *516 Danforth Avenue, tel: (416) 466-8158*. Dinner daily. This is the best restaurant on the Danforth. Great traditional Greek seafood, plus dishes derived from the Greek islands and staples like an elegant moussaka. Try the leek pie or a selection of dips to start. A good variety of wines as well.

Splendido $$$$ *88 Harbord Street, tel: (416) 929-7788*. Dinner Mon–Sat. The atmosphere is charged, and the California-Italian cuisine is splendid too. Different flavors are combined to create satisfying dishes such as the pan-seared sea bass in a red wine sauce or the lamb rack with red chili-honey-pumpkin seed crust in a cardamom-scented *jus*. Extensive wine list.

Truffles $$$$ *21 Avenue Road (in the Four Seasons Hotel), tel: (416) 928-7331*. Dinner Mon–Sat. Award-winning Truffles is one of the best restaurants in the city. The decor is tastefully elegant. Excellent contemporary cuisine with some unique touches, such as salmon with fricassee and carrot-cumin sauce, or pan-seared duck with shiitake mushrooms and potato cannelloni.

Amaya $$ *17001 Bayview Avenue, tel: (416) 322-3270.* Dinner daily. One of Toronto's superb Indian restaurants. Chef Dinesh Singh Butola's diverse menu features the mild cuisine of North India with specialties such as Harra Kebab Fritters, Savory Chaat and Patrani Machchi (banana leaf wrapped halibut).

Centro $$$$ *2472 Yonge Street, tel: (416) 483-2211.* Dinner Mon–Sat. A wonderfully comfortable but grand space that is ideal for a celebration. The contemporary cuisine, superb and pricey, features the best ingredients – Québec foie gras, Bay of Fundy salmon, Nunavik caribou, and Woolwich Farm goat cheese, in winning combinations. Exquisite desserts as well.

El Jacalito $$ *1500 Royal York, tel: (416) 244-4447.* Lunch and dinner Wed–Mon. A Mexican *taquería* with authentic fare. Banana leaf-wrapped pork or chicken and rich, refried beans with crumbled queso are favorites.

Grano $$–$$$$ *2035 Yonge Street, tel: (416) 440-1986, <www. grano.ca>.* Mon–Sat 10am–10pm. Classic, cheerful and authentic Italian fare with welcoming service. A long-standing favorite with the local neighborhood and with the broader Italian community for its impeccable style and unflagging high standards.

North 44° $$$$ *2537 Yonge Street, tel: (416) 487-4897.* Dinner Mon–Sat. Contemporary, international cuisine in a handsome, soaring space with open kitchen in the rear. Dishes are prepared with infused oils and intense broths using ultra-fresh ingredients. Extensive wine list.

Scaramouche $$$$ *1 Benvenuto Place, tel: (416) 961-8011.* Dinner Mon–Sat. Considered by many to be Toronto's most romantic restaurant, wooing customers for more than 20 years. The organic ingredients are enhanced by intensely flavored reductions and glazes – the bordelaise on the filet mignon, for example, or the natural juices with caramelized cranberry glaze that come with the local squab and seared foie gras. Delicious desserts.

INDEX

Berlitz pocket guide

Toronto

Thirteenth Edition 2009

Written by Marilyn Wood
Updated by Heidi Sopinka
Principal photographers: Richard and Daniella Nowitz
Edited by Lesley Gordon
Series Editor: Tony Halliday

Printed in Singapore by Insight Print Services (Pte) Ltd, 38 Joo Koon Road, Singapore 628990. Tel: (65) 6865-1600. Fax: (65) 6861-6438

Berlitz Trademark Reg. U.S. Patent Office and other countries. Marca Registrada

Photography credits
Richard and Daniella Nowitz/Apa 2 bottom right, 3 top right, 6, 9, 13, 14, 22, 24, 26 28, 30, 36, 37, 38, 41, 42, 43, 47, 48, 58, 60, 82, 84, 85, 86, 90, 97, 98, 101; Jackie Garrow/Apa 11, 18, 29, 33, 35, 39, 40, 45, 49, 51, 56, 61, 62, 73, 81, 89, 93, 95, 104; Image Ontario 65, 66, 68, 71, 74, 77, 79, 80, 94, 102; istockphoto 3 centre right, 3 bottom right, 31; Toronto Tourism 8, 55, 64; Mississauga Heritage 17; Ontario Archives 20; Erling Mandelmann 72; *Head* by Jean-Pierre Larocque (Canada), courtesy of the Gardiner Museum 53

Cover picture: Steve Allen/Brand X/Corbis

Every effort has been made to provide accurate information in this publication, but changes are inevitable. The publisher cannot be responsible for any resulting loss, inconvenience or injury.

Contact us

At Berlitz we strive to keep our guides as accurate and up to date as possible, but if you find anything that has changed, or if you have any suggestions on ways to improve this guide, then we would be delighted to hear from you.

Berlitz Publishing, PO Box 7910, London SE1 1WE, England.
fax: (44) 20 7403 0290
email: berlitz@apaguide.co.uk
www.berlitzpublishing.com